To my Bolivian parents, Doña Nona and Don Carlos Zabalaga, who have provided me the space and warmth to be productive and whose own lives of dedication to truth, justice and the poor are examples for us all. To Padre Gregorio Iriarte, OMI, Bolivia's debt and globalisation expert and my personal 'guru' and friend for 15 years - we also laugh a lot together.

# Contents

## Tables

# Acknowledgements

First, I want to thank my editor at Latin America Bureau, Marcela López Levy, who may well be the most supportive and understanding in her field. Many authors make such public proclamations but I know for a fact that few actually mean it. I do. Thank you, Marcela.

Second, my love and thanks to Lucien Chauvin (who helped me with my first book on the debt crisis, published in 1988) and Enrique (Kique) Bossio. They shared their home with me for three weeks in Lima, Peru, permitting me to usurp their dining room table for the duration, and giving me the mental space and time to mostly complete this work, as well as intellectual feedback when I needed it.

Thanks to the Center of Concern in Washington DC which published my original debt book, *Dialogue on Debt: Alternative Analyses and Solutions*, in 1988 and gave me full permission to re-use any relevant parts now. Would that there had been more to use, but the world economic situation has changed so much that most of this book is new material.

I met Angela Wood of the London-based Bretton Woods Project in January 1999. Ever since then she has been a great source of information and dialogue thanks to email and her own diligence and caring.

London-based CAFOD's Duncan Green (a previous editor at Latin America Bureau) was essential in helping me come to grips with capital flows. Under great time pressures of his own, Duncan nevertheless never failed to answer my emails to him in a timely and informative manner.

Lucy Conger has been a friend and colleague for many years. Our email conversations between Mexico (where she lives) and Bolivia (where I reside) were illuminating, and the articles she sent me on the Mexican and Ecuadorean crises were essential.

John Dillon from Canada's Ecumenical Coalition for Economic Justice (I still fondly think of it as GATT-FLY) is another old friend and colleague. He not only brought me up to speed on the Free Trade Area of the Americas and other timely issues, but also diligently answered all my urgent queries with unprecedented speed. Does anxiety translate on email? John clearly sensed mine and helped to alleviate it.

Steve and Doug Hellinger of the Washington DC-based Development Group for Alternative Development (D-GAP) are other dear old friends and colleagues, who also helped me immensely on various issues. Actually, just knowing they are there helps my psyche on a regular basis. Thanks guys, and remember I'm the original GAP!

Gustavo Esteva in Mexico was invaluable in helping me think through true alternatives to the mess the world economic system confronts. His generosity in sharing his as yet unpublished and other works and dialoguing with me in personal communiqués via email humble me. One of my high school teachers used to say, 'If you need something important done quickly and well, ask the busiest person you know to help.' That's Gustavo. Muchas gracias, compañero.

Oscar Ugarteche has been a good friend for over a decade and usually over a good bottle of wine we discuss debt issues like others might gossip about family – the issue is that dear and close to us both. Oscar generously offered to write the Preface for this book.

The global Jubilee 2000 movement, especially Jubilee 2000 South, must be acknowledged for bringing many issues in this book to the public's attention for the first time. Anna Weeks of South Africa was especially helpful, sending me news and other clippings from around the world on a daily basis.

I must also 'thank' the Internet – without which it would have been impossible from Cochabamba, Bolivia, to have had access to all the people mentioned above, plus many other resources available on numerous web sites.

Finally, I want and need to acknowledge the poor and working class people in the world who have struggled to survive these now almost two decades of 'current' financial crises. May their courage and struggle bear fruit soon so that we may all live in a just and equitable environment.

Many resources were used in preparing this book. Most of the statistical data are not footnoted since they came from widely available sources such as newspapers, international organisation publications, etc. When the same statistic was found in more than three reputable sources it was deemed to be in the public domain and therefore not require specific citation. Many pieces by other authors have been included in edited and translated forms, however, I take full responsibility for the views expressed in this book, unless otherwise noted.

GAP
Lima and Cochabamba, May 2000

# Preface

Close attention is being paid by many political, social and economic leaders around the world to a common concern. The world order, the existing institutionality, yet another lost decade in Latin America, wholesale disaster in Africa, and the frailty of democracy in all these countries has led, together with major changes in Eastern Europe and Asia, to mass international migration from the South to North.

Corporate-led globalisation and economic and financial rules of the game oppressive to debtor nations are not making the world a better place to live in. This time round, it all started with the 1982 debt crisis. Eighteen years after the debt crisis was initially declared, George Anne Potter brings us a book to remind us that the problem remains at the core of international economic events. The issues of whose problem it really is, and why, and how it can be solved as well as the consequences of doing nothing about them, are at the core of this work.

For two hundred years we have observed recurrent debt crises in the developing world. Every time interest rates go up in London or New York, raw materials prices fall. There is clearly a debt cycle. There is ample evidence that when the national income of countries falls, payment difficulties arise and they end up in a moratoria which is solved two decades later, through changes in the international rules of the game. Such is the history of international credit in Latin America. In the last decades of the 20th century, it has been the fate of Africa too.

It is impossible to understand the financial developments of the 20th century without understanding that the richest countries were the largest and remain the largest borrowers in world financial markets. Private and public sectors from the West, or the North, as it they are now called, are the largest borrowers. In 1931, Germany was the largest single public debtor in the New York Stock Exchange, with 60% of the bond market there. In the early 1920s, Great Britain held so much debt to the US due to the First World War that it was subject to analysis in the British Parliament under the guidance of Lord Colwyn. He concluded that there was a link between slow economic growth in Britain, transfer of savings, depressed consumption and paying foreign debt on a large scale. Which is the reason why Maynard Keynes later suggested that an international monetary conference should be held to solve the questions of international stability. Various debts were forgiven by the United States and Great Britain in order to give support to European countries under the stress of depression and war, circa 1945. There were no conditions, merely the considerations of circumstance. Germany's interwar debt was given a substantial slash in 1953 and the loans from the Marshall Plan were turned into grants with the additional consideration that a trade surplus was required in order for Germany to meet the remaining payments at a rate of interest down from 6.5% to 2.5%.

Only two countries have reneged on their bonds in history: the Soviet Union and the United States. The rest have had to recognise past debts and past mistakes at some point or other. Due to the United States' unpaid bonds problems in the London Market, and their unwillingness to reach an agreement, the United Kingdom sought an international board of arbitration at the League of Nations in the late 1920s. This initiative was vetoed by the US Congress when it arrived for ratification with the argument was that there had been a referendum held in Mississippi in 1852 and that the population had voted against paying the debt because they did not know how it was hired nor how it was used. This was later incorporated as part of the Constitutional amendments of 1890 in the US

It can certainly be said that there are two measuring sticks, one for rich countries, another for the poor. One for credit relationships amongst leading nations and one for relationships between leading and developing nations. What cannot be said, however, is that the aim of achieving international stability for the development of capitalism was obtained through the creation of the International Monetary Fund (IMF). It could be argued that as long as there were fixed exchange rates, world economic growth remained stable – a time still referred to as the Golden Years (1946-1970). It could also be argued that US surpluses flooded Europe with dollars that could not return to the US or inflation would have boomed, in the 1960s. This is the origin of the Eurodollar and the Eurodollar market. The unpegging of the dollar from gold in 1971 at the Smithsonian meeting no doubt is responsible for the financial boom which followed. There is evidence that it was accompanied by major changes in the theoretical framework in which the international, i.e., the leading nations, developed from then on. From 1972 onwards, all theoretical developments have been orientated towards the financial and institutional arenas. Keynes was thrown out with the bathwater, baby and all. The marginal efficiency of capital became the major point of concern.

The result was that Latin America and Africa were flooded with cheap loans. Some, most, will argue this derived from the oil price increase. But oil prices were raised for a reason. It may well have to do with the devaluation of the US dollar between 1971 and 1973, after it was unpegged from the value of gold, which was sharp in terms of the European currencies and the Yen. The world was flooded with devalued dollars. The theoretical change led to an institutional change. Institutions had to adjust to the new rules of the game they had to administer. The IMF became useless, as it could no longer ensure stability among leading nations. It had to change in order to become useful again. And so it did. It was no longer the insurer of fixed exchange rates but the advisor and lender to developing nations undergoing balance of payments stress due to the oil price rise, at first, and the fall in raw materials prices, later.

Having failed to regulate economic crises in rich countries, it was reassigned as the international advisory agency for developing countries for the benefit of private bankers and western nations. This did not last long. The 1980s are paved with their repeated failures. Paris Club agreements under IMF guidance failed repeatedly, leading to endless negotiating rounds. It is worth asking if the process was done only in order to impose increasing conditions on the borrowing nations. Only then did the new role of promoting international capital become clear. International capital would be the solution to the national crises of developing nations. In order to do this the critical debt problems had to be solved. They were tackled at the Paris Club and later through the Brady Plan which transformed private bank loans into long-term bonds. These were meant to be the definitive solutions to the debt problems of Latin America. Once in place, in 1991, the IMF Executive Director announced the crisis was over – for the creditors, of course – and life continued with new rules for the expansion of international capital.

The problems remained at the debtors' end. Economic reforms were said to bring about fast economic recovery. Bolivia was the first trial country and it is still awaiting its fast economic recovery, fifteen years later. Meantime, African nations continue their decline. The new rules were not only *not* providing for growth, but incomes were and are falling for the poorest. The weight of the debt continued to depress growth. But it ensures the transfer of resources from poor countries to the rich, for which the word should be plunder. Were the problems really solved in 1991? Not at all. Are things much better in Latin America and Africa? Inflation was reined in but growth did not return. Some international investment arrived due to privatisation schemes. But new real investment? Hardly any. And then along comes June 1997 with a sharp retraction of capital flows, the Asian crisis, derived from export income problems and devaluation.

We begin the 21st century with the hope that the pressing problems for humanity will be solved, that greed will not get in the way of common sense and humanity. Potter's book is good in giving an overview of the debt problem as it stands and provoking readers into seeing the problems have not gone away. But then, she can provoke even when she is not writing.

Oscar Ugarteche
Lima, June 2000

Oscar Ugarteche is a Peruvian author with a Master's degree from the London Business School and 25 years working on debt issues. He is currently writing a history of debt between leading nations and the relationships between them and the developing nations. In 1999 his *Arqueología de la modernidad: El Perú entre la globalización y la exclusión* was Peru's best selling book. He is based in Peru and currently advises the Jubilee 2000 Coalition. He is Director of SUR, a research institute in Lima.

# Chapter 1
# Introduction

## Why another book on debt?

When I was first approached to write this book my reply was immediate: 'We don't need another book or article or treatise on the debt crisis! There is so much out there already.' The editor replied, 'Yes, there is, but not all the arguments are available in one place and what is missing is the vision to convey what it means about global economics and the future of development.' I considered her response and realised she might be correct. Before agreeing to this undertaking, I consulted Padre Gregorio Iriarte in the same vein, and he concurred that all the information is out there (indeed proliferating thanks to the Internet), but that he also thought it was not available in a consolidated fashion. Originally, Marcela and I thought to ask another friend, Peruvian debt expert, Oscar Ugarteche to co-author with me. But Oscar had other commitments on his plate, and proposed a reader of sorts, bringing together others' works on diverse but related aspects of the debt/financial crises in an edited and synthesized fashion. That is largely what this book has turned out to be. Much of it is edited and sometimes translated (by the author unless otherwise stated) from existing articles and reports (with full acknowledgement), brought together to give the bigger picture.

Besides the two bookend cases of typhoid I survived at the beginning and end of this six month project, the biggest challenge by far was the fast changing situation in the international financial institutions – International Bank for Reconstruction and Development (World Bank), International Monetary Fund (IMF), World Trade Organisation (WTO) – and civil society's response, culminating with the millennial Jubilee 2000 campaign. And the pace does not let up. In April 2000 civil society was once again on the streets in Washington D.C., as it was in November 1999 in Seattle during the World Trade Organisation meeting, to express its discontent. Specific demands include that the World Bank and IMF cancel all current debts owed to them; that these institutions cease imposing structural adjustment and pay reparations to those communities in the South that have borne the brunt of such policies; that the World Bank group cease providing advice and resources to private sector investors; and more democracy within the IFIs. There is certain to be more to come.

## Debt in the new millennium

A decade after the publication of my previous debt book, *Dialogue on Debt: Alternative Analyses and Solutions,* two things stand out – what has changed in the profile of the crisis, and what has fundamentally stayed the same.

Among the significant changes is a new geographic focus. In the 1980s, Latin America was the central concern of most analysts, activists and policy makers. With Brazil and Mexico, the two largest Southern debtor countries, teetering on the brink of economic collapse, the region received the lion's share of attention. Now, at the beginning of the new millennium, the even poorer African continent is in the limelight (see below). Accompanying this shift, the more progressive (some would say radical) responses to the crisis from civil society are also coming from Africa, rather than Latin America, by and large. The vanguard has shifted and Latin Americanists need to seriously analyse the African debt situation to better understand their own evolving reality. This book will only allude to aspects of the African situation as it directly relates to Latin America, but the web sites at the end of the publication will suggest where readers can go for more Africa debt crisis information.

Another geographic change is in the industrialised North. The Asian so-called economic miracles of the 1980s, including the NICs (newly industrialised countries, such as Taiwan, South Korea, Singapore and Indonesia) and Japan, have been through the Asian crisis. The impact of the Asian crisis on Latin American economies has been profound and will be examined.

Finally, pundits at the end of the 1980s saw US economic and political hegemony on the wane. At the turn of the century, the opposite is true.

The debt crisis of the 1980s led to a serious crisis in private banking, especially in the US, which now seems to have been corrected. Both private (commercial banks) and public creditors (World Bank, IMF, regional development banks, governments) are now openly and seriously not only talking about debt relief (writing off loans) but actually doing it in comparatively significant ways. This was anathema a decade ago.

The formal trappings of democracy are now the norm throughout the South rather than the exception, as they were during the 1980s. Debt riots are much less frequent and use of force to contain impoverished populations' protests is less common. Of course, popular protests are also significantly fewer, as labour unions have been decimated throughout Latin America by neo-liberal economic policies. Poor and working/middle class people are not necessarily better off, but they are less organised than before and putting their energies into survival rather than protest. Sources of conflict in the

2

1990s include the US-sponsored war on drugs in the region which has replaced anticommunist and economic-related violence.

The worldwide Jubilee 2000 movement is a notable exception in terms of civil society participation in calling for an end to inequality. Latin American debt expert and social commentator Gregorio Iriarte believes that the global Jubilee 2000 movement is the largest ever in history on any issue (environmentalists and feminists might disagree), yet it has certainly mobilised more people on a development issue than any before it.

Finally, what would an analysis of the 1990s be without discussing globalisation, which was already well on its way before, but codified as the millennial change? In the 1980s, respected analysts and activists seriously discussed even partial Southern de-linking from the dominant Northern paradigm. That notion now seems as obsolete as cradle to grave welfare.

## What remains the same

Despite the changes mentioned above, some positive, some not, there is little that is fundamentally different regarding the debt crisis of the last twenty-odd years. Discussions regarding terms of trade and financial flows, intrinsic to globalisation, are considered more widely than a decade ago, but few analysts bring all the issues together. Well-meaning Northern NGOs continue to call for debt relief to be additional to development assistance for poverty reduction, but little emphasis, other than popular participation, seems to be invested in critiquing the now decades-old development model. Poverty reduction (improved health, education, social services) served up as the panacea is pure rhetoric without regard to poverty's fundamental causes. The international financial institutions (IFIs) and Northern government creditors continue to exact structural adjustment conditionalities as part of any debt relief amidst diminishing aid. Taking trade and investment into account were the combined and related concerns of civil society on the streets of Seattle against the World Trade Organisation in late 1999 and out in Washington against the World Bank and IMF in April 2000.

What fundamentally has not changed is the economic (and political) elites' refusal to consider true structural changes over token reforms. Likewise, many of the Northern NGOs and poverty/debt alleviation campaigners continue to work within the very system that perpetuates unjust inequalities. Writing off chunks of current unaffordable debt today, without fundamental changes to the global economy, will only result in a new debt and development crisis a decade from now. Many, if not most, people and activists in the South understand this, because they live it, while many of their Northern

## Globalisation

'Some concepts come to define entire economic policy eras. For the 1990s, "globalisation" will be recorded as the dominant theme [ ]While carrying different connotations for different people, globalisation encapsulates both a description of changing patterns of world trade and finance, and an overwhelming conviction that deregulated markets will achieve optimal outcomes for growth and human welfare. Seldom since the heyday of free trade in the 19th century has economic theory inspired such certainty and never has it been so far removed from reality. [ ] Poverty, mass unemployment, and inequality have grown alongside the expansion of trade and foreign investment associated with globalisation. [ ] In the developing world, poverty continues to increase in absolute terms, and the gap between "successful" and "unsuccessful" countries is widening. In the industrialised world, unemployment has reached levels not witnessed since the 1930s and, in some countries, income inequalities are wider than at any time this century.'

Watkins, 1997

colleagues seem to be stuck in the same 'tactical/strategic' debates of a decade ago.

Finally, I still sense a serious lack of effort to bring poor and disenfranchised people from the North and South together in joint analysis and efforts of common interest. If globalisation is as dominant as we are led to believe, then the poor and working/middle classes in the North have more common self-interest with the poor and working/middle classes of the South, than they have with their own and Southern power elites.

## The dangers of globalisation

Associated with these changes, Bolivian globalisation and debt expert Gregorio Iriate has identified the following list of cautions:

(Edited from Iriarte, 1999)

• Worldwide, corruption is on the increase and more difficult to curtail,
• The nation state has been weakened, and with it 'democracy' and traditional political party influence,
• Labour movements around the world have been decimated,
• Fundamentalism, including overt racism, is on the rise; 'positive' ideologies in decline,
• There is an ever increasing polarisation of wealth,

- Capital and transnational corporations have more power than governments,
- Despite the end of the Cold War, military spending is up 35% since 1992 (it is now some US$7.8 billion a year, equal to nearly half the world's population's income),
- Illicit activities such as drug dealing and related money laundering is increasing,
- Crucial technologies, especially information technology, are increasingly controlled by fewer people,
- Neo-liberal economic policies have reached nearly global ascendancy, to the detriment of the majority of the world's population.

## Human problems

The global debt and financial crises of the 1990s are *people-made problems*. This is the most essential fact to understand about one of the most complex set of issues confronting the world economy today. They are human problems because of the disastrous effects on the poor and working classes caused by the massive debts accumulated decades earlier and neo-liberal economic policies designed to keep the indebted in debt bondage. They are human problems because economic management is decided by people and these decisions are not naturally occurring events, currently in favour of profit, not people. Hunger, poor health and education, decreasing employment opportunities and loss of sovereignty – these are the consequences of national economies struggling with debt and globalisation.

### Africa needs debt cancellation, not more IMF programmes

(Edited from *50 Years is Enough*)

Sub-Saharan Africa, so rich in human and natural resources, remains the poorest region of the world economically. Half of its people live in poverty, and in many countries economic conditions have been getting worse for the last twenty years. The greatest barrier to economic recovery is the region's overwhelming debt burden, which amounts to about $230 billion ($203 billion if South Africa, with its anomalous history, is not included). Thirty-three of the region's forty-four countries are designated 'heavily indebted poor countries' by the World Bank; most of the rest nearly qualify for that ranking. Creditors, chiefly the International Monetary Fund (IMF) and World Bank, impose harsh conditions, and investors shy away from countries with unsustainable debts.

Much of the debt accumulated by African countries was built up during the 1970s, a time of reckless lending by Northern banks and international agencies, and was agreed to by undemocratic governments. In many cases, the population of the borrowing country realised little benefit from the loans as the money disappeared in failed infrastructure projects, corrupt schemes, or unwise investments. The debt has continued to grow since then as governments take out new loans to pay off old ones.

In 1996, sub-Saharan Africa (minus South Africa) paid $2.5 billion more in debt servicing than it received in new long-term loans and credit. The IMF alone has taken over $3 billion out of Africa since the mid-1980s. It is the poor people of the indebted countries, those who benefited least, who end up paying the bills through scarce resources diverted to debt servicing, and through the effects of the IMF/ World Bank austerity programs. Average real wages decreased in twenty-six out of twenty-eight African countries surveyed during the 1980s. Cuts in health spending have led to an increase in infant mortality: African children

**African debt in perspective**
Jubilee 2000, UK
The countries of Africa and Latin America have suffered the most because of unpayable debt. Today it is Africa which bears the greatest burden of international debt. Although the size of Latin America debt surpasses that of Africa, it amounts to an inverse proportion of the continent's Gross National Product (GNP).

*Total external debt*

**Latin America:**     US$546 billion

**Sub-Sahara**

**Africa:**     US$214 billion

*Total external debt as percentage of GNP*

**Latin America:**     36%

**Sub-Sahara Africa:**     83%

**Chains around Africa: the slavery of debt in the world's most impoverished continent**
Adrian Lovett, Jubilee 2000, UK
• For every US$1 received in aid grants in 1996, Africa paid back US$1.31 in debt service
• Africa shoulders 11% of the developing world's debts, with only 5% of the South's income - twice the burden of any other region in the developing world
• The IMF took out US$600 million more from Africa than it put in during 1997
• The prices of exports from Africa fell by 1.2% on average each year from 1990-96 and the effect on export and import prices combined makes Africa one third worse off than they were in 1980
• If Africa's export prices had kept pace with import prices since 1980, Africa could have repaid all its debts one and a half times over

accounted for about 40% of infant deaths worldwide in the year 2000. Debt is what subjects African countries to the mandates of the IMF and World Bank. Debt is what diverts resources from health and education spending.

The external debt burden of sub-Saharan Africa has increased by nearly 400% since 1980. External debt per capita for the region (not including South Africa) is $365, while Gross National Product (GNP) per capita is just $308. The external debt for the region (again excluding South Africa), at some $203 billion in 1996, represents 313% of the annual value of its exports. Debt servicing for the region amounts to about 20% of its export income. Africa spends four times more on debt interest payments than on health care.

The above figures are clearly unsustainable, which is why debt relief is now discussed. But debt relief without structural global economic changes in trade and financial flows, and a new sustainable development model (different from the current neo-liberal dominant paradigm) will do little to help Africa or the rest of the South.

# Chapter 2
# History of the current crisis

Conventional contemporary wisdom dates the current international debt crisis to 1982 when Mexico (the second largest Southern debtor) announced it could no longer service its debt. Wiser analysts maintain that the real roots of the problem predate this event by a decade when the first OPEC (Organisation of Petroleum Exporting Countries) oil crisis hit the world in 1973 awash as it was with devaluated dollars.

Even then, it was hardly a new phenomenon. The crisis in the 1990s was but the latest symptom of a much older structural problem, codified by the Bretton Woods System in the 1940s, but whose historical roots are to be found in the colonial and post-colonial economic system of goods and financial transfers. Foreign debt is nothing new to the South. It is a cyclical problem, directly connected to the recurring crises that plague the Western capitalist world model – now commonly referred to as 'globalisation' an 'neoliberalism.'

## From colonialism to 'independence'

Many countries have lived with a foreign debt since colonial times. Brazil, the largest Southern debtor, defaulted on its external debt in 1899, only to be in the same positions in 1987. Mexico negotiated its first foreign debt as an independent country in 1823. Argentina went into debt even before independence when it borrowed money from England to fight Spanish colonial rule.

Creditor nations have used military force to collect their debts in the past. In 1915, US Marines landed in Haiti and stayed for almost a quarter of a century, ostensibly because the Haitian government had failed to pay its debts.

In the end, however, the debt crises of the 19th and early 20th centuries were not solved until creditors agreed to sweeping write-offs and the remaining restructured debts were bolstered with new net lending accompanied by high growth rates and expanding international trade markets.

## The First and Second World Wars – the US and Europe

US debt policy after First World War was different from that adopted after Second World War. The Treaty of Versailles, ending the First World War, obliged Germany to pay more than US$30 billion of war reparations to the European allies, who at the same time owed the United States US$20 billion. The US lent Germany the money it needed to pay the allies so that they in turn could repay the US. However, with the Great Depression, the US stopped making loans and a new approach was adopted in 1929, which allowed Germany to pay smaller amounts over a longer period of time. By 1931, however, even this payment 'reschedule' was impossible to meet and the US was forced to declare a moratorium on the allied war debt. In 1932, the Europeans formally cancelled Germany's reparation obligations, and with the exception of Finland, the allies stopped paying the US Within Germany, popular bitterness at being made to pay for the war was one of the factors which destabilised the economy and contributed to the social upheavals which Nazism exploited. The instability which ensued was predicted by a young economist in 1919, Maynard Keynes, who was to play a major role in a different approach to post-war debt in 1945.

After the Second World War, the US implemented the Marshall Plan which pumped in US$13 billion between 1948-52 to reconstruct Europe in an effort to keep out the Russians as the Cold War began to take shape. At the same time, the current global economic model was established under the Bretton Woods system (see Chapter 3).

## The 1980s debt crisis

By the 1960s, most Latin American countries had been politically independent for almost a century and a half and the African continent was slowly emerging into post-colonial independence. Both continents inherited an economic system based on exporting cheap raw materials and importing expensive manufactured goods from ex-colonial rulers. Political independence did not bring economic sovereignty with it.

The US and Europe were preoccupied with the Great Depression of the 1930s, the Second World War in the 1940s, and Europe and Japan's post-war reconstruction in the 1950s. It wasn't until the 1960s that the North began to look South (to the then called Third World). It was time to 'develop' the 'less fortunate' ex-colonies. In order to do this, the South would have to 'modernise' to some extent (industrialise certain sectors), or as became fashionable in development economics, creates the conditions for the 'take-off' of capitalist industrialisation. The US was ready to supply foreign aid no longer needed in Europe and Japan. Moreover, US and European

9

companies were also finding it attractive to head South where they could avoid taxes while finding cheap 'surplus' labour. Northern banks followed shortly afterward to service the companies and lend them the money needed for new investments. Some analysts call this first period of the current debt crisis the 'competitive entry phase,' which coincides with the origin of stateless 'Eurodollars,' that is, dollars deposited outside the US to earn interest which are then used as loans by commercial banks. When the Eurodollar market replaced the gold standard in 1971, banks found a largely unregulated market in which to conduct business. Spurred on by the OPEC countries' $375 billion surplus, the Eurodollar market grew ten-fold from 1973-83, from $100 billion to over $1 trillion. This represented an average 25% growth per year compared with only 4% growth in world trade and productive investment over the same period. The difference was used for short-term speculation and loans to Third World countries. Neither governments nor IFIs have influence over this supranational currency, the control of which is in the hands of private banks. Through the 1980s the banks escaped government regulation over these funds, including minimum reserve levels, no deposit insurance and virtually no reporting requirements. It was this money from which was to come the bulk of 'Third World' debt. The money transfer mechanisms were already in place for the OPEC crises of 1973 and 1979.

Before entering into those crucial 'petro' events, it is important to understand several other phenomena which were also taking place in the 1970s. The unique position of the US dollar, which replaced the gold standard in 1971 as the international medium of exchange, allowed the US to begin accumulating, first a small, but then a growing domestic debt to finance the Vietnam War and increasing trade competition from Europe and Japan. This further enhanced the Eurodollar and world banking reserves increased eleven-fold. A larger money supply led to higher inflation which lowered interest rates and increased the incentives for Southern government borrowing.

Meanwhile, then US President Richard Nixon had not only unilaterally removed the US dollar from the gold standard, but he also devalued the dollar twice in the early 1970s without prior consultation with the IMF (see Chapter 3). The international system of fixed exchange rates was replaced by floating ones, leading to rampant speculation. Pundits have dubbed Eurodollar markets the era of 'casino capitalism,' which continues today (see Chapter 4). In effect, the dollar became the global currency of choice for international banking, in spite of no longer being backed by the gold standard, which means its value depends on the confidence of the finance community. Thus, while Northern international financial institutions and politicians found it convenient to blame the 1980s debt crisis on the OPEC oil price hikes of the 1970s, that explanation only partially clarifies the situation. The uncertainty of the system resulted in a tremendous amount of resources, including unrestrained lending to the South, being diverted into financial speculation.

At the same time, multinational corporations (MNCs) were continuing to increase their Southern expansion to take advantage of cheap money and labour, especially women. This industrial relocation was paid for by commercial bank loans, which increased by 550% from 1973-1980. Thus the 'development' supported in the 1960s by Northern government grants or long-term, fixed interest rate loans, in the 1970s was increasingly funded by commercial loans repayable at variable interest rates over shorter periods of time. By the time the 1973 oil crisis materialised, many Southern countries were dependent on continued oil imports to keep their new fuel-dependent industries running.

When the OPEC countries increased the price of oil in 1973, the newly developing Southern countries continued importing this fuel but now had to borrow money to do so. OPEC revenues were deposited in safe Northern banks which then had to lend these new and increased funds out at higher interest rates in order to eventually pay back the OPEC countries and make a banking profit themselves. It is estimated that one fourth of all new loans to the South during this period was generated directly by the OPEC money surplus. *Business Week* called it the 'debt economy.'

When the second OPEC oil crisis happened in 1979 it was significantly different in an important way. Unlike the earlier period when the North maintained growth with inflation, this time around it adopted fiscal policies which slowed both, resulting in fewer Northern markets, at lower prices, for an ever increasing Southern production of goods. The debt service burden of Southern countries rose spectacularly just when they needed more money to pay higher oil prices. The deteriorated terms of trade with industrialised and oil exporting countries is one of the most important reasons for the 1980s debt crisis and reflects age-old colonial inequalities between North and South.

## The 1980s – the lost development decade

By the time the second OPEC oil crisis hit in 1979, the stage was set for the ensuing recession which was characterised on the one hand by severe US anti-inflationary policies, leading to increased interest rates and decreased imports from the South. On the other side, the developing countries had accumulated huge debts from loans squandered on inefficiently managed and badly conceived development projects, coupled with macroeconomic policies leading to inflation and overvalued currencies. Rounding off the scenario, great chunks of the loan funds were appropriated outright by Southern political and economic elites who then exported the borrowed sovereign money to their own private bank accounts in the North in what is known as capital flight. One analyst suggested that 70% of all loans to the eight largest Southern debtor nations returned to the North in this manner.

High interest rates coupled with inability to repay (not properly calculated by lending banks) precipitated the Mexico loan repayment moratorium of August 1982. With large debts accumulated in the previous decade and now coming due, the South also faced the worst 'terms of trade' (the relation between the price of what a country sells to the price of what it buys) in 30 years. In 1981-82, Southern export earning losses of US$100 billion contributed to unprecedented balance of payment deficits. For the first time in the $20^{th}$ century, developing countries had to borrow just to service their earlier debts. This 'round-tripping,' whereby banks issued new loans just so debtors could service old loans, was accompanied by higher interest rates in the North which exacerbated an already bleak situation.

In the mid-1970s the median real interest rate averaged 1.6%, but by the early 1980s, due to the Reagan Administration's tight money, monetarist policies, interest rates exploded to an average 11%, with some rates as high as double that. No wonder US commercial bank lending to Southern countries increased more that 300% between 1978-82 alone! The result was devastating for Southern borrowers. By 1983, 40% of all Southern loans were tied to floating and ever higher interest rates, where even a 1% increase was estimated to cost an additional US$4-5 billion annually in Southern debt servicing.

It is estimated that between 1980-81 alone the external factors of increased interest rates plus declining terms of trade resulted in a US$141 billion increase in Southern debt. These two years set the stage for the rash of debt repayment rescheduling which would become the norm after the 1982 Mexico crisis. By the end of 1983, higher interest rates would account for 50% of all developing country debt service increases. There was a very high human, economic and political cost for the 'breathing space' rescheduling provides.

Governments and commercial banks consider default bad for the world economy and private business since it could jeopardise the international financial system by impairing their profits and viability as businesses. Thus, when Mexico announced in August 1982 that it could no longer service its debt, the US government pressured the commercial banks and the IMF to extend new loans to Mexico to help it keep up payments. The Mexican crisis resulted in the dramatic increase of IMF influence, whereby Northern donor governments doubled their funding to this institution, but only for highly conditional loans. Over the next six years close to 200 different case-by-case debtor country negotiations ensued. The golden age of IMF structural adjustment agreements had arrived. As a result, Southern debtor countries paid out more in debt service than before and the actual net flow of capital was from South to North (see below).

By 1983, 79% of new Latin American loans were used to pay interest on old debts and two thirds of all export earnings covered the rest. Whereas the 'blame' for the debt problem of the 1970s may be shared by creditors and sovereign borrowers alike, in the 1980s the major responsibility for the deteriorating situation lies clearly with the Northern nations, their commercial banks and the international financial institutions they control. What started out as a liquidity problem had become a solvency problem – or the inability to pay.

## Liquidity vs. Solvency

There is an important difference between the two types of financial problems which may be faced by developing countries.

A liquidity problem arises when a country does not have enough foreign exchange to meet the debt service payments and other obligations due at a particular point in time, although it would ultimately be able to meet its obligations if they were delayed long enough. If a country has a liquidity problem, its main need is for more foreign exchange going into the economy to meet its immediate obligations.

A solvency problem arises when a country would never be able to meet its obligations, however long they were delayed. Even if creditors were willing to defer the country's obligations, or lend more money to finance them, the obligation in the future would increase. Insolvency problems can only be tackled by cancelling existing obligations (e.g. through debt cancellation), or by improving their terms either directly (e.g. by lowering interest rates or by deferring obligations at interest rates well below the market rate) or indirectly (e.g. by providing grants or highly concessional loans to meet the obligations).

Woodward, 1998

The Northern governments and their countries' banks refused to admit there was a Southern debt crisis until the IMF began to run out of money. In September 1985 then US Treasury Secretary James Baker acknowledged the problem when he proposed the Program for Sustained Growth, which would have both the IMF and commercial banks significantly increase their lending to Southern countries. Whether this came when it did because the US had woken up to a long-standing problem, or in response to Cuba's Fidel Castro's call for a Southern debtors' moratorium and Peru's Alan García's declarations in the same vein, is debatable. Either way, Baker's plan did not take hold, since Northern commercial banks reduced lending rather than increased it. The 'freeze phase' of the debt crisis had begun. Since 1984 the South has been a net exporter of capital to the North. For Latin America alone, the net capital outflow between 1982-87 came to US$125 billion. For the South as a whole, the net transfer of funds between 1980-86 totalled almost US$650 billion, more than half of that in interest payments alone. Yet at the end of the millennium, the South was more in debt than ever (see Chapter 5).

The first sign that Northern creditors realised that Southern debt had become impossible to pay came in early 1988 when the US Treasury backed Mexican debt bonds into the indefinite future. Despite the poor commercial results of this deal it was significant in that the Northern creditors for the first time recognised that Southern debt could not be paid in full. However, their actions again had more to do with looking after their own interests, as letting the second-largest Southern debtor default might spiral out of creditors' control and endanger repayments generally. The timing for departing from Baker's full repayment plan was not coincidental. Northern commercial creditor banks had begun to write off all or parts of their Latin American debts in light of the fact that some dozen Southern countries had simply stopped paying their debt service altogether. Northern creditors were happy for any scheme which involved even partial voluntary payments by the debtors.

Throughout the 1980s one of the glaring differences between Latin American and African debt (Asian countries were less debt ridden) was that most Latin American debt was owed to Northern commercial banks while African debt was largely in the hands of European national and international agency creditors (WB, IMF, African Development Bank). Over the years, several European governments and Canada had written off portions of their loans to the poorest sub-Saharan African countries. The US, however, steadfastly rejected such initiatives until the mid-1980s. The French government announced immediately prior to a G-7 summit that it was cancelling a third of its loans to the poorest Southern debtor countries, after which the Reagan Administration no longer opposed debt relief but continued to withhold its own endorsement and adoption of such a policy solution.

Perhaps the most salient element at the end of the 1980s debt crisis was that no Southern debtor government fully repudiated any of its debts, despite the increasing recognition that much of it had already been paid through usurious interest rates, deteriorating terms of trade and capital flight. Northern creditor governments, commercial banks and international agencies, by and large, continued with rescheduling and conditioned macro-economic strategies which contained the crisis and averted major disruptions of the capitalist financial system by imposing the burden of adjustment almost entirely on the poor in the debtor countries. Nonetheless, at the end of the 1980s the key Northern creditors were beginning to scramble to find self-interested and often conflicting 'solutions' in the hopes of diffusing the crisis or at least the costs to themselves.

Meanwhile US taxpayers were bailing out the creditors, for example Chicago's Continental Illinois. Having decided to expand in 1976, by 1981 it had become the country's sixth largest commercial bank. But bad loans to the Third World as well as declining US economic sectors meant that by 1982 Continental Illinois found itself holding lots of worthless debts. In 1984 overseas depositors withdrew $15 billion when they sensed the bank's imminent collapse. Fearing a panic the FDIC (Federal Deposit Insurance Corporation) and Federal Reserve stepped in with $1.5 billion and 'convinced' other banks to contribute $0.5 billion. Stressing the 'cooperative' nature of the bailout was imperative to maintain public confidence in the banking system.

Thus we enter the 'exit phase,' where commercial banks and some Northern governments began to try to bail out. At this point the creditors, divided in their self-interest, showed no capacity to formulate any comprehensive policy changes, while the debtors faced a deteriorating world economy. It had become clear to those committed to a just solution that the only acceptable outcome must involve a fundamental change in inequitable South/North and class relations and a new development paradigm. The last decade of the millennium was unfortunately better at formulating questions than solutions to these problems.

## The 1990s – the found development decade?

In the early 1990s, the international development and financial communities expressed great optimism regarding the Latin American debt crisis. Indeed, at some point mid-decade the crisis was declared to be over. There was much discussion about the booms in financial markets, new inflows of foreign investment and the return of domestic capital from abroad. As the British weekly, *The Economist,* wrote in 1992, 'the re-emerging markets in Latin America have become hot business,' and 'nowhere are the celebrations of life after debt bigger than on Wall Street.' Net inflows of new capital jumped from about US$8 billion a year in the late 1980s to an annual average of US$60 billion during 1992-94, decreasing to about US$30 billion in 1995 (CEPAL). Other reports on economic and social conditions emphasized the 'long awaited recovery …generated by the reform process [have] stimulated

15

private investment, encouraged a boom in the equity markets, and attracted substantial financial flows from abroad' (Inter-American Development Bank). Despite the Mexican financial crisis of 1994-95 and its repercussions there and elsewhere, much of the international community continued to laud the positive recovery of the region.

While the debt crisis might have been over for the Northern creditor banks (in late 1999, the US banks Citigroup, JP Morgan and Bank of New York tripled their earnings over the previous year alone), it most certainly was not over for people in the debtor countries. Most Latin American countries continued to confront a development crisis throughout the decade. Although macro-economic indicators in the early-mid 1990s showed improvement, social well being (human indicators) did not (see Chapter 6).

## Players in the international debt crisis

| Major categories | Sub-sets |
|---|---|
| People | • Southern poor and working class<br>• Northern taxpayers and working class<br>• Northern and Southern elites<br>• Civil society movements |
| Debtor countries | • Middle income (emerging) and advanced developing countries with debts to the commercial banking system and multilateral and bilateral official loans (Latin America/Caribbean, Asia)<br>• Highly indebted poor and other low income nations with mostly multilateral and bilateral official debt (mostly Sub-Sahara Africa and some Latin American)<br>• Transition economies (eg Central & Eastern Europe) |
| Creditor countries (Paris Club) | • US, Canada, Western Europe and Japan |
| Group of 7 (G-7) | • Canada, France, Germany, Italy, Japan, UK, US (and sometimes Russia as G-8) |
| Private commercial banks (London Club) | • Large money banks |
| Multilateral Financial Institutions | • Primarily the World Bank and IMF, but also regional development banks (e.g. Inter-American Development Bank) |

Mexico clearly illustrates this vulnerability. Its mid-90s financial crisis led to more structural adjustments, greater unemployment and deteriorating living standards. Real wages fell by 25% in 1995 and 18 months after the crisis, 'living standards are lower than they were in 1980's according to the *The Economist.* By the time the Brady Plan, named after a US Treasurer began to be implemented in the 1990s, the international banking crisis had largely been averted as debtor countries proceeded to pay their inflated bills under IMF (and increasingly World Bank) structural adjustment conditions. Commercial banks were deemed sufficiently 'secure' by now that small amounts of debt relief were negotiated for the first time since the crisis began in 1982.

The other significant aspect of the 1990s has been increased globalisation. The rest of this book will deal with aspects of the debt, trade, financial transfers, development and globalisation in the 1990s.

## The Brady Plan

The Brady Plan, formulated by the U.S., was announced in 1989 and introduced as a way to go beyond the 1980s debt crisis. It was designed to provide restructuring of mostly Latin American countries' debts with Northern commercial banks via U.S. government guaranteed bonds with different maturation dates. In 1990, Mexico was the first country to restructure its debt in this way, and between then and 1993, 14 Latin American countries obtained new loans valued at US$25 billion through Brady Bonds sold on the global market. Terms differed in each case. Mexico, Brazil, Argentina and Venezuela hold 85% of these debts. In recent years, Brady Bonds have become among the most negotiable debts in emerging financial markets (see Chapter 5 below for further discussion of the 1999 Ecuador Brady Bond payment moratorium crisis).

Note: See Bello, 1999 and Hanlon, 1998b in Bibliography for more historical information.

# Chapter 3
## The Bretton Woods System

To seek just solutions to the current economic malaise one must first understand the evolution of the global system which has perpetuated these inequities from its foundation in 1944 at the Bretton Woods Conference in New Hampshire, US. This was a gathering of 700 participants from 44 nations assembled to plot the economic course of the post-Second World War, non-communist world. Two major institutions were created at the meeting: the International Bank for Reconstruction and Development (World Bank) and the International Monetary Fund (IMF).

### Historical overview

The problems which prompted the creation of the Bretton Woods system can be seen as early as the 1920s as the United Kingdom failed to regain the global economic dominance it held before the First World War. As the UK faltered, the US, with a growing and newer industrial base, gained rapidly on the global economic scene, but in a markedly different way. Unlike England before it, the US did not at first emerge as a single hegemonic power, but rather as a force which promoted competing blocs of economic strength. Nations turned inward and economic isolationism (protectionism in today's vernacular) became a cornerstone of the world wide economic collapse of the 1930s, and would eventually fuel the Second World War.

As the Second World War approached, western economies were in disarray. The US economic collapse of 1929 sparked a subsequent depression throughout the industrialised nations of Europe. The international economy of the 1930s was a combination of falling production, bankruptcies and high unemployment coupled with the unwillingness, at the time, of any one nation to take the lead toward recovery. The US, especially, prolonged the crisis by raising taxes and adopting severe protectionist tariffs. This in turn prompted similar policies in Western Europe.

In light of these circumstances, John Maynard Keynes, one of the leading British economists of the time, pushed for an international conference which would promote economic cohesion by establishing an international economic institution and a world currency. While Keynes saw economic depression and war as a result of nationalistic proclivities, he also believed in national ﬧnomic self-reliance, arguing that international trade should be limited to ﾧs which could not reasonably be produced domestically. His argument implied that any possible inefficiencies that might result from trade restrictions would be more than compensated by gains in domestic employment.

The election of F.D. Roosevelt as president in 1932 marked the shift in the US from a protectionist economic power to that of a leading world creditor. Using a Keynsian model, Roosevelt took the US off the gold standard and began to rebuild the US economy by pouring millions of dollars into domestic infrastructure and creating jobs through programmes known collectively as the New Deal. By the late 1930s, the US was poised to become the world's leading economic and political power. The Second World War was just the push needed to accomplish the task. What the New Deal started, the Second World War completed, bringing the US out of the Great Depression and into world economic prominence.

As the Second World War drew to an end, Keynes and then US Assistant Treasury Secretary Harry Dexter White began discussions which would lead to the Bretton Woods Conference. They both agreed on the need for a global economic institution coupled with an international currency not tied to the gold standard. Keynes maintained that reliance on gold was the cause of unemployment and a contributing cause to possible future economic collapses.

The Bretton Woods Conference opened with Keynes as chair and White as vice-chair, both bringing to the meeting a model which challenged the economic foundations at the time. By the end of the Conference, however, both Keynes and White would abandon their original goals and adopt the conventional proposals of their respective governments.

As the Conference drew to an end, two major agreements emerged:

1.  The creation of the World Bank and IMF.

2.  An agreement among participating countries to fix the value of their own currencies in terms of gold or its US dollar equivalent and the acceptance of gold/US dollar as the international payment for trade goods.

Keynes immediately criticised the new system. First, the World Bank and IMF were too small to handle global economic problems. Second, the dependence on a gold/dollar standard would eventually strangle the smaller nations. In retrospect, Keynes' criticisms proved to be prophetic in light of the current debt crisis as the gold standard didn't work for long and the IMF especially has proven too small time and again to sustain its own model.

In the years immediately following the war, the Bretton Woods Institutions (BWIs) were in no way large enough to cope with the massive reconstruction of Europe and Japan. The intact US economy, fuelled further by post-war reconstruction, quickly became the dominant force in the realm of international trade. Its industrial strength was export-oriented with little need to depend on imported goods. What eventually rejuvenated the world economy was not the strengthening of member country economies by the World Bank and IMF, but the advent of another conflict – the Cold War, which pumped billions of US dollars into Europe and Japan to contain communism. The US Marshall Plan (named after Secretary of State George Marshall) guaranteed Western Europe billions of dollars of aid (over US$12 billion to Europe and Japan). In contrast, the combined loans of the World Bank and IMF during this period were less than US$3 billion.

## The World Bank

Membership of the World Bank (IBRD) is contingent upon three principles:
- a member nation must first become a member of the IMF
- each nation must pay 1% of its membership fee in gold or US dollars – this money is used at the discretion of Bank officials
- each nation must pay a percentage of its membership fee in its own domestic currency

IBRD loans are non-concessional, that is, they charge market interest rates. These loans are made to middle income countries.

In the late 1950s, the Bank established a lending institution for its poorest members, the International Development Association (IDA). IDA makes loans on soft terms to the least developed countries (LDCs) set as those with per capita incomes of less than US$1,000 per annum. IDA loans have very low (½ -¾%) interest rates and very long repayment schedules (up to 45-50 years) during which only minimal interest is paid.

In the 1960s, the Bank began to supplement its development project portfolio with loans to finance imports, such as oil. To qualify for these monies, borrowing countries needed to present austerity plans to demonstrate fiscal responsibility in reducing foreign deficits. This was the precursor of the structural adjustment lending to come.

In the 1970s, the Bank broadened its loan portfolio to include projects which generated foreign capital. The problem with these projects was that little of the investment 'trickles down' to the poor. By 1987, 29% of World Bank loans went to export agriculture and development finance companies, while only 2.8% went to health, education and nutrition combined.

In the 1980s, a majority of Bank loans were contingent upon reducing domestic social programmes and promoting hard currency (dollar) earnings export-oriented projects to help maintain debt service payments. The poor were thus trapped by increasing unemployment, lower wages and a reduction in social services. First under the leadership of A.W. Clausen and then under President Barber Conable, the Bank began highlighting what it perceived as structural weaknesses. Structural Adjustment Loans (SALs) or Programs

(SAPs) were introduced in 1980 and were specifically geared to increasing foreign exchange through austere (some would say draconian) macro-economic policies rather than building the needed domestic human and physical infrastructure necessary for true development. In the late 1980s, the Bank claimed that no more than 25% of its lending would be in the form of SALs. A decade later, in 1998, this had risen to 39%, and a year later (supposedly because of the Asian crisis and its affects on Latin America as well) SALs made up 65% of the Bank's lending portfolio. Bank officials 'hope' to reduce this to 30-40% in the next millennium.

## Structural adjustment

(Excerpted from Hanlon, 1998a)

The major components of SALs are:
- free trade policies
- mobilisation of domestic resources through tax reforms
- reduction of the public sector (cut social spending and reduce government jobs)
- privatisation of state owned and operated enterprises (even if profitable).

In 1983, SALs were strengthened by the introduction of Sectoral Adjustment Loans, designed specifically to increase export production earnings for debt service payments.

The Bank's HIPC (Highly Indebted Poor Country) initiative was introduced in 1996 and began to be implemented in 1997. It applied to 41 of the world's poorest countries, mostly in sub-Saharan Africa, but three years later only four countries (Uganda, Bolivia, Guyana and Mozambique) had met the complex conditions required to receive debt relief under this mechanism (and only Bolivia and Uganda had actually received any debt relief). Up to 80% of an eligible country's debt could be cancelled by bi- and multilateral creditors combined. Many advocates for a just solution to the debt crisis considered HIPC to be the most important step toward resolving the crisis in nearly two decades, since it fundamentally accepted for the first time that:
- any long term solution requires debt *cancellation* and that all lenders, including multilaterals, must participate
- there must be enough relief to release countries from perpetual debt bondage
- this means a reduction in creditor imposed conditionalities

Despite these advances, the first three years of HIPC I (see below for discussion of HIPC II) demonstrated that it simply wasn't working. It was

*[handwritten margin note: Only 4 countries]*

21

slow, secretive and inadequate in scope. For example, a sufficiently poor and indebted country needed to wait three years under World Bank and IMF scrutiny and conditions before being eligible (the Decision Point) and another three years for full debt relief (the Completion Point).

Since the 1980s, the World Bank has increasingly demonstrated its interdependency with the IMF. It is sometimes even called the 'tax collector' for its fellow institution.

Even the World Bank's own ex-senior vice president and chief economist, Joseph Stiglitz, was highly critical of what he and others call the Washington Consensus, made up by US economic policy officials, the Bank and IMF. The Washington Consensus only sought to increase GDP, whereas 'we seek to increase living standards – including improved health and education [ ] We seek equitable development which ensures that all groups in society enjoy the fruits of development, not just the few at the top. And we seek democratic development.' Stiglitz undermined virtually every pillar of structural adjustment and HIPC I by asserting that:

- moderate inflation is not harmful and may be helpful for long-term economic growth,
- some budget deficits can be useful, especially in crucial areas such as education, health and necessary physical infrastructure,
- macro-economic stability is the wrong target when productivity is down/unemployment is up,
- the benefits of privatisation are exaggerated and its costs underestimated – efficiency not ownership is the key,
- unfettered markets are not necessarily better than no government intervention for human and technological development,
- liberalisation of financial markets has high risks, like the Asian crisis.

## The wages of liberalisation

Vice President Stiglitz was put on ice by the Bank for some time after making the above observations and resigned in December 1999. In an interview with the *International Herald Tribune* and commenting on the Asian financial crisis, Stiglitz maintained that it was 'the international financial markets that were at the root of the problem.' In a speech to the American Economics Association in January, this same expert said: 'Capital market liberalisation has not only *not* brought people the prosperity they were promised, but it has also brought these crises, with wages falling 20 or 30 percent, and unemployment going up by a factor of two, three, four or ten.' Since then, Stiglitz has accepted a post as chair of a Wall Street investment firm that specialises in emerging markets, the very ones he criticized above.

The IBRD has two other component organisations, the International Financial Corporation (IFI), which supports private sector projects in developing countries, and the Multilateral Investment Guarantee Agency (MIGA), which guarantees foreign investors against certain risks involved in investing in the South. The next chapter will deal with foreign investment as it relates to debt and development, and therefore to the World Bank and IMF.

## The International Monetary Fund

The IMF was the other major institution to emerge from the Bretton Woods Conference and was envisioned as a means by which member nations of the non-communist, post-war world could obtain loans to stabilise their devastated economies. Unlike the World Bank, the IMF does not make loans for development projects but was conceived with restructuring and organising the western capitalist economic system to which its members belonged. Originally, the IMF had five basic mandates:

- to promote international economic and monetary co-operation
- to foster and encourage growth in international trade
- to encourage members' stable national currencies (in order to facilitate international trade)
- to provide funds to reduce members' foreign debt
- to shorten the time frame for members' foreign debt repayments.

Each member nation pays a fee to the Fund, partially in its own local currency, with the remainder paid in US dollars or gold. As a member nation there are certain rules to be followed. First, members must have economic policies which encourage free trade and growth. Second, economic policies must be such that stability can be measured in terms of IMF conditions. Finally, domestic economic policies and trade laws must be consistent with other members' (see next chapter for more in depth trade discussion).

IMF policies can be traced in great part to US pressure. The Roosevelt Administration guaranteed the pre-eminent role of the US in establishing international financial policies as the IMF charter gives the country which contributes the largest percentage of funds the most control over policy and funding decisions. In effect, this continues to give the US a near veto power, which it is reluctant to release. When Japan, for example, has urged to be allowed to contribute more to the Fund, this has been rejected.

Originally, the IMF was established to assist member nations in financing *temporary* deficits and establishing 'solid' monetary and trade policies. These policies have been repeatedly reformulated since the early 1950s, with the most dramatic changes resulting from the 1980s debt crisis. In 1986, the SAF Structural Adjustment Facility (SAF) was created, then supplemented in late 1987 by the Enhanced Structural Adjustment Facility (ESAF) for the poorest

23

countries. ESAF loans carried minimal ½% annual interest rates and had to be repaid within ten years. These parallel facilities were designed to encourage (coerce?) the LDCs, especially those with high debt ratios, to undertake draconian macro-economic structural adjustment programmes to improve their balance of payments positions. As a result, the IMF began to essentially guarantee Southern nations' loans primarily for debt servicing, export trade and foreign investment.

Moreover, the IMF maintains that the main cause of Southern nation indebtedness is similar in most developing countries: government inability to control spending. Southern countries are largely perceived as profligate adolescents unable to manage their own finances, so the IMF (and increasingly the World Bank) requires strict budget tightening programmes (structural adjustment) before loans are granted. These programmes typically result in increased multinational foreign investment in previously sovereign sectors of the economy and reduction in basic social services for the vast majority of the population – the poor. IMF (and again, increasingly World Bank) loan conditionalities include:

• currency devaluation (to make exports cheaper) and trade liberalisation to encourage increased imports

• reduced government spending, especially in social services (health, education, infrastructure) and elimination of government subsidies which benefited the poor most

• privatisation of state enterprises and elimination of government investment subsidies, encouraging foreign investment over local firms

• reduction or elimination of labour rights and benefits, including wage freezes and often massive unemployment.

As the remaining working class and poor struggle to survive with lower (or no incomes) and evaporating social services, the disparity between rich and poor (both North and South and internally) has become an ever harder chasm to breach (see Chapter 6). At his late 1999 resignation speech, then IMF Managing Director Michel Camdessus unusually candidly admitted that, 'As IMF director, I obliged those countries seeking our help to submit to major (macro-economic) surgery when six aspirins could have brought the same results.' Pundits claim that Camdessus resigned because of the IMF's incompetent handling of the Asian and Russian financial crises (see next chapter).

In February 2000 an interim IMF director was named with the knowledge that the new director would be another European. The first candidate was rejected by the US and another German, Horst Hohler, was finally agreed upon after a group of African governments and Japan proposed their own nominees. The whole procedure has demonstrated how undemocratic the

24

whole process is, with no public accountability. The IMF has set up a committee to improve the process.

## The language of conditionality

IMF and World Bank conditions have a language all their own. At the IMF, binding conditions are known as *performance criteria* and non-binding conditions are known as *structural benchmarks*. The IMF also has a category known as *prior actions,* those needed to be taken prior to receiving the loan. The World Bank calls its prior actions *triggers*. Triggers are conditions that a government must fulfil in order to maintain or increase access to World Bank loans. IMF and World Bank conditions overlap, since about 64% of the World Bank's IDA loans are conditioned on compliance with IMF loan conditions. So many trigger actions are in fact IMF performance criteria reinforced through World Bank lending instruments. Conditions which have the potential of being highly controversial among civil society actors are still frequently kept secret.

Bread for the World Institute, 1999

The IMF has now undertaken its second generation of reforms which focus on good governance, ever deeper structural reforms, banking sector improvements and capital account liberalisation (though in early 2000 it admitted that some capital controls may be needed temporarily in some cases, but not as a basic principle – see next chapter). The World Bank is also increasingly concerned with corruption, justice systems and other non-economic specific areas in applying its conditionalities. One study showed that IMF ESAF programmes contained more conditions than SAF programmes, but that ESAFs performed less well. Even the IMF admits 'that high conditionality programmes do not generally do well' (Lockwood and Wood, 1999). Moreover, debtor countries and much of their population view conditionalities as seriously undermining their sovereignty. Nonetheless, IMF and World Bank conditions continue. The latest initiatives from the Bank and IMF, described below, represent a token attempt to address some of the serious criticisms surrounding conditionalities now for well over a decade.

## Millennium changes?

In January 1999, World Bank President James Wolfensohn announced the Bank's new Comprehensive Development Framework (CDF), addressing shortcomings of the current development *process* (but not challenging the neo-liberal paradigm in any way). The CDF is intended to highlight the interdependency of a country's social, structural, human, governance,

25

environmental, economic and financial aspects. The main (and new to the Bank) attributes of the CDF are:

•  Host Country Government Ownership – the borrowing government, in consultation, will prepare its own development programme which the Bank will then review and 'approve.' This approach not only supposedly addresses sovereignty concerns mentioned above, but also should result in better programmatic execution.

•  Partnership with Civil Society and the Private Sector – a new step toward host country ownership and improved planning and implementation.

•  Donor Co-ordination – All international bi- and multi-lateral donors are expected to co-ordinate their funding rather than compete for sexier or high profile programmes, in the interest of filling all the gaps. To this end, as well as civil society and private sector participation, a development framework – or matrix – has been designed. However, there is disagreement among and within institutions as to whether the matrix should be regarded as a management tool or as a strategic planning tool. So far the former and less revolutionary approach seems to apply.

•  Country Selectivity – refers to the acknowledged need to work with those governments which have both the technical ability and political willingness to participate. A good macro-economic environment (neo-liberal development model) and good projects/programmes are also required.

•  Transparency – both the Bank and borrowing countries are notorious for not sharing lending information and programme design/implementation/ evaluation documents with the public. This is now to be corrected, but it remains unclear if the Bank or the borrowing country is responsible for making such information available.

•  Better Data – acknowledges the need for better data, especially on social sector indicators.

•  Holistic – macro-economic (neo-liberal) and social/structural concerns are to be considered jointly.

•  World Bank Culture – finally, recognition that Bank staff themselves need to revise their approach to one which is more participatory and socially concerned (poverty alleviation).

In June 1999 the G-7 (G-8 when Russia is included) countries met in Cologne, Germany. It was striking how the government leaders there adopted (co-opted?) language from NGO advocates, including 'faster, broader and deeper debt relief.' Although they may be the same words, they do not have the same intent, as questions remained regarding conditions for qualifying for relief and financing for HIPC II. 'The Cologne G-7(8) meeting reinforced controversial IMF and World Bank macro-economic and structural conditions for debt relief rather than conditions that focus on ensuring that debt relief is channelled toward prioritised local human development concerns' (Bread for the World Institute, 1999). It still remained for the World Bank and IMF in September 1999 to come up with specific implementation criteria.

In anticipation of the G-7 Cologne Summit, Harvard University economist (and previously structural adjustment guru) Jeffrey Sachs, gave testimony to the US Congress calling for 100% debt cancellation for at least half of the HIPC countries, echoing Jubilee 2000 's (see Chapter 8) call for 'a shift from sustainable debts to sustainable development.' He also urged that 'the IMF be taken out of the lead in the debt reduction process in the poorest countries' and 'return to its core role as a monetary institution.'

In the autumn of 1999, the World Bank and IMF held their first ever joint annual meetings. Several breakthroughs in the nearly two-decade old debt crisis were alleged to emerge. Most significant were a new joint approach to poverty reduction in relation to debt and the World Bank's emphasis on the private sector's role in development. Months later, World Bank president James Wolfensohn had this to say:

## Let's hear everyone and get on with imaginative solutions

By James D. Wolfensohn  28 January 2000, World Bank President
From the *International Herald Tribune*

It has lately become routine for international development institutions to interrupt euphoric talk about the magic of the new global economy with stern reminders about the world's poorest. We need those interruptions, perhaps nowhere more than at high-profile events such as this week's annual gathering of political, financial and business leaders in Davos, Switzerland. Despite all the efforts of governments, official institutions and non-governmental organisations, we will never significantly reduce the number of hungry children unless we forge dynamic coalitions of governments, civil society and the private sector to build a global economy that benefits all people. We need these coalitions now more than ever. Despite years of relative peace and prosperity in industrialised countries, global poverty is getting worse. Some 1.2 billion people now live in extreme poverty. More troubling still is the massive and widening gap between rich and poor. In Brazil, for example, the poorest 20 percent of the population earn just 2.5 percent of the country's income, and the richest 20 percent control nearly two-thirds. This is not just an extreme case. Alarming ratios are seen in countries as different as Colombia and Niger, South Africa and Russia. This cannot go on indefinitely without a backlash.

## Poverty Reduction and Growth Strategy Papers/Program (PRSP)
## – the New ESAF?

After the 1996 internal IMF evaluation and the 1998 external review, it was 'found' that at least 75% of ESAF programmes performed badly and the IMF announced a new poverty approach, the PRSP. With the stroke of a pen, ESAF was abolished with PRSP emerging phoenix-like from the ashes. The PRSP is to be a joint World Bank and IMF plan, mutually approved and supervised on a country-by-country basis. Although debtor country government and civil society input are called for, the IMF and World Bank retain veto rights. Funding for the G-7(8) Cologne Debt Initiative is to be administered by the IMF and Bank through the HIPC II/PRSP (ex-ESAF) trust fund and makes the IMF key in setting the terms and conditions of debt relief. The mandate and power of the IMF is significantly enhanced.

To be eligible, debtor countries must prove that funds saved from reduced interest payments will be transferred to social spending, especially in health and education, and that this is done within the framework of 'sound macro-economic policies and good governance.' While this new collaboration between the Bank and IMF has moved the latter into poverty alleviation rhetoric, the Bank is also increasingly seen as the handmaiden for the Fund. The two institutions have identified six new areas of overlapping responsibility: tax policy and administration, transparency, corruption reduction, legislative reforms, trade policy and debt. In theory, the World Bank's CDF (Comprehensive Development Framework – see above) will also have resonance in IMF approaches.

## HIPC II

The enhanced HIPC II framework provides for deeper and quicker debt relief within this supposedly more transparent policy. Now, debt relief will result in a 150% debt to export ratio (HIPC I had a 200-250% ratio) or a fiscal ratio of 250% (previously 280%) debt to revenue. Debt relief will be calculated on actual need, not projections, with more interim relief than before. In theory, the IMF's and World Bank's vision is shared more now with the debtor government and civil society in a consultative process concerning poverty (CDF and PRSP). Eventually, it is envisioned that poverty reduction and transparency criteria will next apply to all IDA countries and then middle income debtors, not only those that are HIPC eligible. Some middle income countries, notably Brazil and India, have already expressed their disapproval of HIPC II, claiming it will take money away from them in the short run and also that the forced civil society participation, transparency and other innovations are nothing more than new conditionalities. It remains unclear whether traditional IMF macro-economic criteria or World Bank poverty reduction initiatives will reign supreme if they are in conflict, but most bets are on the IMF getting their way.

HIPC II countries are required to prepare a PRSP (poverty reduction strategy), which may delay some of their entries (Decision Point) into this new debt relief mechanism. Exceptions will be made, as in the case of Honduras and Bolivia, if governments have a supposed clear anti-poverty and pro-civil society record. The Completion Point, when the major portion of debt relief is actually provided, is now 'floating' rather than a firm 3-6 years, and dependent on proven debt reduction strategy implementation and macro-economic stability. 'In the period between Decision and Completion Points, the enhanced HIPC II framework will provide increased interim assistance in order to partially reduce debt servicing, such that more resources can be freed up for poverty reduction. Under HIPC I, use of debt service payment 'savings' for social spending – especially in health and education, were encouraged – a debt of honour – but not contractually binding. Countries which have already made progress through HIPC(I), such as Uganda, Bolivia, Guyana and Mozambique will be re-assessed for retroactive action in order to benefit from the new framework' (OXFAM International, 1999).

Directly after the IMF/World Bank Annual meetings in September 1999, US President Bill Clinton announced his support for 100% cancellation of US bilateral debt to HIPC countries. Considerable Congressional opposition remained, though US Treasury Secretary Larry Summers announced in December 1999 a US$12.7 million cancellation of Bolivian debt and additional funds for other debtor countries, but not as much as Clinton requested. Canada had already agreed to a similar write-off and the British government announced its cancellation of 100% of its bilateral debt to the world's poorest 25 countries. If all 41 HIPC II countries were included such debt cancellation would cost the United Kingdom some US$3.24 billion – 96% of which is owed to the Export Credit Guarantee Corporation and a mere remaining 4% to DfID, the UK ministry of development. These debt cancellations were more than anticipated during the June 1999 G-7/8 meetings in Germany, but were also to be discounted over a 20 year period. The UK also announced it was reducing its contributions to the World Bank and IMF for debt reduction purposes as the downside to their bilateral bounty. While the amount of money actually involved may not be that great, out of the G-7/8 we now have the US, Canada, and the UK doing something, with France on the way with its announced US$1.5 billion cancellation of all trade credits accrued before 1990 by the 40 poorest countries, toward pressuring for fuller debt relief. Japan and other big bilateral creditors remain an enigma.

For 15 years, Bolivia, South America's poorest country (Haiti in the Caribbean is considerably poorer) has been the test case for IMF/World Bank and bilateral debt negotiations and structural adjustment deals. As one of the first HIPC I and HIPC II country beneficiaries, it is informative to analyse the details.

Table I Estimated Bolivian debt service before and after HIPC

(millions of US$)

|  | 1995 | 1996 | 1997 | 1998 | 1999 | 2000 | 2001 |
|---|---|---|---|---|---|---|---|
| Unpayable debt service before HIPC I | 528.3 | 349.6 | 356 | 352 | 363 | 367 | 380 |
| Debt service paid before HIPC I | 327.7 | 349.6 | 356 |  |  |  |  |
| Debt service due after HIPC I |  |  |  | 355.2 | 292 | 300 | 307 |
| Debt service due after HIPC II |  |  |  |  | 201 | 205 | 205 |

Bread for the World Institute, 1999

As of February 1999, it was announced that Bolivia would benefit from US$1.3 billion in debt relief over the next 15 years, under HIPC II. The catch is that the government of Bolivia must develop a viable anti-poverty plan including civil society participation and transparency, (see below).

## Cancelling multilateral debt

(Excerpted from Ambrose, 1999)

The response of the World Bank and the IMF to the debt crisis was the Heavily Indebted Poor Countries (HIPC) Initiative of 1996, revised in 1999. The ostensible aim of the program is to determine which countries have 'unsustainable' burdens, then to caucus with each country's creditors to reduce the debt across the board until it is 'sustainable.' The program seeks to ensure that countries do not run up 'unsustainable' debts again by insisting that beneficiaries demonstrate a proven commitment to 'sound economic policies' the IFIs' usual euphemism for SAPs.

To qualify for HIPC, a country must complete three years under an IMF-designed SAP. Even after that hurdle, the country must fulfil a further three years bound by another SAP before relief on multilateral debt is granted. At that time, all creditors will give matching relief to reduce the country's debt to a 'sustainable' level. The new version of HIPC allows for the granting of relief as soon as the debtor country completes its first SAP, though the debt can be reinstated if the second SAP is not fulfilled to the IMF's satisfaction. The cruel paradox is that countries in desperate need of debt relief so they can begin to direct resources to social sectors are required to first demonstrate their willingness to make things worse by depriving their people of health care, food subsidies and education.

The new version of HIPC seeks to ensure that debt relief will effectively reduce poverty through the Poverty Reduction and Growth Strategy Papers Program (PRSP), the new name given in September 1999 to the IMF's Enhanced Structural Adjustment Facility (ESAF). The IMF claims that the new programme relies on government and civil society to come up with their economic recommendations and that their primary goal will be poverty reduction. But civil society organisations in Uganda and Tanzania, two of the first countries to embark on the PRSP, report that the IMF still expects to provide the basic economic framework, with civil society filling in minor details and signing off.

There are indications that the PRSP will simply become an additional stumbling block; for example, the US government's dissatisfaction with Mozambique's and Uganda's Poverty Reduction Strategy Papers has delayed their debt relief packages. The PRSP is widely viewed as both a cynical public relations ploy and an expansion of the IMF's power, since, at Washington's insistence, the IMF now claims the right to oversee poverty programmes.

There are other problems with HIPC's complex formulas. 'Debt sustainability' means how much a country can repay without going broke. In many cases, countries are not paying all their debt servicing bills because they simply haven't got the money. But the definition of 'sustainability' is a harsh one: a debt-to-export ratio of 150%, meaning that a country's outstanding debt is one and a half times a large as annual exports. In practice, this means about 15% of a country's annual export income flows out of the country in the form of debt payments (capital plus interest).

Outright debt cancellation, the only humane solution to the most impoverished countries' debt crises, would undermine the policy leverage now exercised by the IFIs. The absence of debt burdens would make countries more creditworthy and thus less dependent on the IFIs' conditioned loans. In the wake of Hurricane Mitch's devastation in Central America, Treasury Department officials gave 'loss of leverage' as their reason for refusing to consider comprehensive debt cancellation for Nicaragua and Honduras. President Clinton's September 1999 pledge of 100% forgiveness of bilateral debts owed the US by the most impoverished countries was important for

31

breaking that taboo. But it appears that his offer will be made only to countries graduating from HIPC and committed to ongoing structural adjustment.

## Abracadabra says the IMF

(Excerpted from Block, 1999)

In order to fund its part of HIPC II, the IMF proposed and passed a motion that it should conduct off-market gold sales. It is important that these revenues be only used for HIPC II and not for the re-named ESAF – PRSP. Such sales could not go forward without US Congressional approval, which was granted in some measure in December 1999. The original idea of outright gold sales was nixed by the US and gold producing countries (especially in Southern Africa) because of its potentially deflationary impact on gold prices world wide.

Instead, it (the IMF) has come up with a plan to 'revalue' its gold. It is a feat of magical accounting and works like this: the IMF carries its gold at the 1973 value of US$48 an ounce, dating back to when the gold came to the Fund from its member nations. A big difference between that and the current market price of US$255.

The IMF will sell at least 10 million ounces of gold at the prevailing market price to countries, such as Mexico , which owe the IMF money from past loans. These countries would then buy IMF gold the day before loan payments are due and then repay the loan the next day with the same gold…

These transactions would give the IMF a profit of US$207 an ounce, or about US$2.1 billion. The gold also never actually leaves the IMF vaults and would never hit the open market so the price of gold should remain unaffected.

Once the gold is sold, the Fund would return US$48 per ounce to its general resource account and then transfer the profits to a trust fund (for HIPC II).

Opponents say they are against the IMF's increasing global role and this plan should be rejected at least until all questions are answered about the possible misuse of IMF loans in Russia and Indonesia – and assure critics that this is not a way to bolster up the newly renamed but discredited ESAF fund.

mixed 2

## IMF policy shifts?

(Excerpted from OXFAM International, 1999)

In December 1999 the IMF made its first gold sale under this scheme to Brazil, which paid off a portion of its debt the next day to the IMF, on schedule.

Other interesting initiatives which were and were not discussed/resolved at the first joint World Bank/IMF Annual Meetings in late September 1999:

*Amending the IMF's Articles:* to include the liberalisation of capital movements (see next chapter) as part of the Fund's mandate was tabled for further discussion. Many analysts believe that such capital liberalisation was a major contributing factor to the Asian crisis.

*The Global Financial Structure:* this was less discussed at this meeting because the global financial crisis is now deemed over and Asian recovery well under way by the Washington Consensus. New debt relief mechanisms (see above) involving the Bank and the Fund predominated.

*The Private Sector:* Ecuador's decision to default on its Brady Bonds (see Chapter 5) brought the issue of sovereign insolvency to the forefront. The IMF agreed to continue lending to Ecuador while it is in arrears to private creditors. It signified a Fund policy shift and provided a signal to capital markets that it wants the private sector involved.

*G-20:* This new forum was announced just before the meeting and will supplement the G-7/8 by focusing on the future of the international financial system in a globalised economy. Members are the G-7/8 plus Argentina, Australia, Brazil, China, India, Mexico, Russia, Saudi Arabia, South Africa, South Korea, Turkey and representatives from the EU and the IMF/World Bank.

### Bolivia – the perpetual test case

Bolivia is the poorest country in South America and one of the poorest in the Western Hemisphere. This ignoble attribute has also made Bolivia vulnerable to Northern influences (the US-led war on drugs for one), including debt related machinations by the World Bank and IMF.

In 1985-86, Bolivia underwent one of the first and most severe SAPs to date, designed by the now contrite Harvard economist, Jeffrey Sachs. According to the current IMF director in Bolivia, 'We often need to overshoot on purpose to get what we want.' He also admitted that ESAF in Bolivia was successful in getting new laws passed, but that poverty had not been alleviated. The Bank's own 1998 Country Assessment Strategy (CAS) candidly states that our 'overall impact on poverty reduction has been limited.'

The Bank's original 1998 Comprehensive Development Framework (CDF) in Bolivia, as one of the first countries to apply it, also proved to be less than comprehensive. The government itself, some bilateral donors, the IMF and civil society were excluded from its preparation. Not surprisingly, there was lack of detail regarding which projects and reforms various 'partners' were contributing to. There was no clarity on how crosscutting issues such as gender, human rights, poverty and the environment would be incorporated, nor how certain contradictions among different parts of the matrix would be addressed.

Since the CDF was largely based on the government's pre-existing National Dialogue (ND), it would be fair to say that there is adequate Government of Bolivia (GOB) ownership of the matrix, although the area of greatest concern to the GOB – the war on drugs – is excluded from the CDF. Civil society did participate, in a restricted fashion, in the ND in late 1997, so both the Bank and GOB claim they have fulfilled that criterion. However, NGOs and other sectors of Bolivian civil society criticise that when the actual CDF process was underway in early/mid-1999, they were invited to participate at the last moment, given a day or so notice, many key players were excluded (only one group from outside La Paz was invited) and almost all documents provided by the Bank were only available in English. When the Bank Representative was asked about the lack of participation and even common courtesy, she replied that the initiative was foisted upon her by Washington.

The funding Consultative Group (CG) meeting for the CDF was held in Paris in mid-1999, rather than in Bolivia, as recommended by the Bank's own Partnership Initiative, to allow broader civil society and private sector participation. Civil society and private sector participation remains ad hoc and the Bank has no apparent systematic strategy for engaging these sectors.

The GOB, with the help of a Bank official from Washington, presented the draft Poverty Reduction Strategy Paper in December 1999, still based on the two year old (non-participatory) National Dialogue. A 'new' National Dialogue followed in 2000. The Catholic Church/Jubilee 2000 held its National Forum in late April 2000 based on local, regional and departmental fora with broad civil society participation – iterating its distrust for the government's plan and ability to convoke civil society. Even the country's business sector has declared its unwillingness to participate in the government's initiative. The results of the Jubilee 2000 National Forum will feed into the government's National Dialogue final document for presentation in Washington by the end of 2000 in order to qualify for HIPC II the same year.

The IMF prepared an interim Policy Framework Paper based on this process so that by June 2000 Bolivia was eligible for the Decision Point entry of HIPC II and post-ESAF Poverty Reduction and Growth Facility funding. No specific social indicator targets are required for Decision Point money disbursements, but performance criteria would be related to future tranches of PRSP funding. However, standard macro-economic criteria will apply from the beginning. The IMF director gladly confirmed that of course macro-economic policies come first and that the PRSP is indeed ESAF with a new name.

The Bank's CAS (1998-2002) will be refined in light of the PRSP but they will not conduct a poverty impact assessment and there will be no formal public reporting of changes made, leaving transparency a problem at all levels. 'The Bank has lacked the instruments to monitor and evaluate the poverty reduction impact of its operations in a systematic way' (CAS, 1998). The Bank's chief economist in Bolivia said they are still not sure how to assess social impacts and that it might take another 15 years to do so!

In summary, poverty alleviation, civil society participation and transparency remain at the margins in this, the first test case for all the new initiatives emanating from the Bretton Woods institutions.

## World Bank Board discussion of Bolivian PRSP

### Summary

The Board approved Bolivia's request for a Decision Point under the enhanced HIPC II, with a floating time horizon for the Completion Point. They also accepted the interim PRSP as a basis for working to a final PRSP, based on a national dialogue, which would be the main prerequisite for reaching the completion point.

There were many criticisms, however, of the interim PRSP. While acknowledging Bolivia's good track record in macro-economic management, there was a general feeling of unease that poverty remained high despite relatively rapid economic growth. The candour of the staff assessment was noted and appreciated. Criticisms of the interim PRSP generally followed many of the points from the staff assessment, and came mostly from the US, France, German and Netherlands chairs. While recognising the 'interim' nature of the I-PRSP, these chairs noted that it:

• was a very descriptive document, not yet a strategy, and needed 'much refining'
• did not analyse the causes of poverty
• needed a better analysis of the steps to reduce poverty
• lacked indicators which could be monitored
• needed to say much more about the priorities, costs and trade-offs of various programmes proposed

• needed to say more about sources of funding for the programme, and the realism of the projected incremental costs (which are twice the amounts expected to be freed up under HIPC II)

• assumed an overly optimistic timing for completion of the national dialogue, and

• did not mention certain key issues, such as tax and land reform.

In addition, members raised concerns about the failure of the previous national dialogue, and the possibility that the next dialogue would also end in failure, and/or would not be sufficiently inclusive of all aspects of society, including all private and public institutions. The Nordic chair suggested that the national dialogue be institutionalised as a permanent body.

In contrast to the Bolivian HIPC scenario, the Uganda case seems more promising, as described below by Uganda Debt Network, a leading civil society organisation.

## Uganda: HIPC experience and development-oriented borrowing
(Edited from Gariyo, 1998)

I am here to represent the Uganda Debt Network, a coalition of Ugandan NGOs, academic and religious institutions, civic and grassroots groups and individuals. The network was formed in 1996 as part of civil society initiatives in Uganda to influence public policy planning and to establish a forum to debate the impact of the external debt burden on Uganda. The network also participated in the campaign for debt relief under the HIPC initiative and is an active member and co-ordinator of the Jubilee 2000 campaign in Uganda. Since 1996, the network has established itself as the foremost advocacy organisation on debt, budgetary policies and poverty eradication initiatives.

Uganda was the first country to become eligible to receive debt relief under the HIPC initiative sponsored by the World Bank and IMF. The country reached the Decision Point in September 1997 and reached its Completion Point in April 1998. As part of the conditionality to qualify for debt relief, Uganda committed itself to spend the money saved from debt relief in the social sector and in the priority areas of education, health, agriculture, water and sanitation. Both Government and NGOs lobbied the World Bank and IMF to accelerate debt relief. Uganda is one of the poorest countries in the world, ranking 160 out of 175 on the United Nations Human Development Index.

Uganda's debt service has been reduced from over US$150 million (before HIPC debt relief) to US$120 million (after HIPC debt relief). The debt relief is expected to provide a saving to government for budgetary spending. Consequently, during the 1998/99 budget, the government committed to increase budgetary spending in education from less than 10% in financial year 1997/98 to over 20% in 1998/99. The bulk of this will be spent on the Universal Primary Education (UPE) program. The government also committed to increase spending in health from less than 3% in 1997/98 to over 7.5% in 1998/99. The bulk of the increased expenditure is to be spent in Primary Health Care (PHC).

The government committed itself to an open audit and to a performance budget. To implement an open audit, the government has established the offices of the Auditor General and Inspector General of Government as independent and autonomous institutions. In addition, the Parliamentary Public Accounts Committee (PAC) and the Standing Committee on the National Economy respectively, scrutinise government spending and budgetary commitments during the financial year.

The Government has also established a mechanism to report to the public, donors and the media on actual spending and the results of such spending. Thus under the decentralisation policy, funds to districts are released on a quarterly basis with full accountability and reports of achievements. This is to ensure that funds released are related to results and according to the public investment plan.

The government budget for the social sector is also based on the priorities identified in the Poverty Eradication Action Plan (PEAP), a program developed in 1996 with the participation of civil society in Uganda. The poverty action plan prioritised education, health, agricultural extension, water, sanitation and feeder roads as key elements in poverty eradication.

The Inspector General of Government (IGG) has also established mechanisms for monitoring public expenditure. A weekly radio program was established on the national radio. In this way, the public can monitor spending by public servants and can write letters if they feel public servants are using public finances for private purposes. Cases are reported and investigated, and reports of the results read on the radio. In addition, a hotline has been established at the offices of the IGG where individuals can report cases of suspected fraud of public finances.

The Public Accounts Committee considers the report of the Auditor General and considers action to be taken. Individuals have been dismissed as a result of recommendations by government. The government established the Ministry of Ethics and Integrity to ensure that government and parliamentary recommendations are implemented. The office also provides political co-ordination for all anti-corruption agencies. It implements political actions recommended by the agencies and parliament.

The Poverty Action Fund (PAF) was established by the Ugandan government to mobilise additional donor resources for spending in the social sector.

37

The PAF was established as a substitute for the Multilateral Debt Fund established in 1995 by donors to provide US$50 to 60 million per annum to the government to be used to pay for debt service. 80% of the PAF resources are from HIPC. Donors provide an extra 20%. Thus government commitment to the PAF has been provided by savings from HIPC debt relief.

The additional resources committed by donors to the PAF are to be used for the construction of classrooms for primary schools under the UPE program of 1997. Under the UPE, enrolment in primary schools has recently increased from 2.6 million to 5.9 million, thus making it necessary to construct extra classrooms. Under the PAF, NGOs have been provided with funding for primary health care programs.

> **Ignoring the costs**
> 'An examination by the Operations Evaluation Department of the World Bank ... found that income inequality increased in half the SAL countries studied and that in most countries with adjustment programmes growth continued to be negligible. The external review of the IMF's…ESAF recognised that adjustment programs entail 'temporary' costs for certain segments of the population….. Nevertheless, a major rewriting of macro-economic and structural adjustment programs has yet to occur.'
>
> Bread for the World Institute, 1999

PAF monies are accounted for separately from the main budgetary expenditure. Every three months, government prepares a report of all incomes, expenditures and results, and presents them to a meeting of donors, NGOs, and the media who can then present their queries to be answered by government agencies. The meetings are chaired by the Permanent Secretary of the Ministry of Finance and are attended by all the line ministries including health, agriculture, water, works (roads), education and the Treasurery Officer of Accounts (the government's Chief Accountant). In addition, regular seminars have been held for Local Government officials to sensitise them to critical budgetary related issues.

The Government and donors have also accepted a suggestion by civil society to put aside 5% of all donor contributions for monitoring utilisation and effectiveness of the PAF, and to include civil society organisations in the monitoring process. The bulk of the money is to be provided to the IGG and Auditor General's Offices to strengthen their monitoring capacity. Civil society organisations are, however, expected to participate in the monitoring process.

Measures have been taken to tackle the high rate of embezzlement of public funds at all levels. Corruption remains rampant and the anti-corruption agencies are being urged to take direct action to increase the participation of civil society in the anti-corruption struggle. The measures also respond to the findings of a study on public expenditure tracking commissioned by government in 1996. The report noted that less than 36% of expenditure in the health and education sub-sectors reach the intended beneficiaries: the health centres, hospitals and schools.

The government has instituted a system of publicising through the print media and on the radio expenditures remitted to districts for education and health. In addition, the money for spending in health and UPE is remitted as conditional grants and is only for spending on specific items: payment of salaries for teachers, lunch allowances for medical staff, money for construction of classrooms. This cannot be diverted for district recurrent expenditure. Districts that do so are denied further funding until they provide accountability.

Uganda has evolved a strategy to invest effectively and efficiently the savings from debt relief. At the moment, the Uganda Debt Network and other civil society members are organising their participation in the post-HIPC monitoring of budgetary processes. The network will also carry out an analysis of loan utilisation as part of the processes of monitoring future borrowing. The network is in the process of building capacity to involve a broad cross section of civil society, such as NGOs, grassroots groups and other civic institutions. This is to ensure that more people get involved in shaping policy planning process at national and local levels.

The Ugandan legal code states that: 'Government shall not borrow, guarantee, or raise a loan on behalf of itself or any other public institution, authority or person except as authorised by or under an Act of Parliament.' UDN will lobby Parliament to put in place a comprehensive Act of Parliament to regulate government borrowing so as to ensure that borrowed resources are put to effective use to achieve economic sustainability. Parliament has already used this provision to reject some proposed loans including a US$21 million loan for capacity building for the Ministry of Agriculture, and recently queried a US$34 million loan for Early Childhood and Nutrition until government clarified the scope and utilisation of the loan. These are some of the examples on how effective Parliament can be if given an opportunity to do its work. UDN will intensify its lobby work in this forum.

# Chapter 4
# Trade and capital

## Trade

Trade and financial flows are now significantly more important in volume and volatility than aid transfers and debt relief.

As a result of the Asian financial crisis in 1997-98, Latin American trade dropped 32% in 1999, demonstrating the region's vulnerability to global economics. The Secretary General of ALADI (the Latin American Association for Integration), has called for a new independent economic model for Latin America. The President of the Andean Development Corporation, bluntly blames globalisation and financial markets for the end of the millennium economic crisis in the region. In light of the Asian crisis, the US now plans to focus more on Latin America as a trading partner: US trade with the region already increased 150% during the 1990s, with Mexico and Brazil leading the pack.

The design of the original Bretton Woods system was to have included a third pillar, the International Trade Organisation (ITO), doing for trade what the IMF did for finance and the World Bank for economic reconstruction. There was insufficient agreement, however, among the architects of the then new world order, (opposition was especially strong from the US), and the ITO was not formed. Nonetheless, two years later, in 1946, the General Agreement on Tariffs and Trade (GATT) was founded, largely by and for the interests of Northern industrialised countries. In 1964, the UN Conference on Trade and Development (UNCTAD) was founded, with Southern interests more in mind, but it never achieved sufficient clout against GATT, or its successor, the World Trade Organisation (WTO), founded in 1995.

Unlike four decades earlier, and with the end of the Cold War, 'by the mid-eighties, trade rivalries with Europe and Japan's rising import penetration of the US market by Third World countries, frustration at the inability of US goods to enter Southern markets, and the rise of new competitors in the shape of the East Asian NICs made the US the leading advocate of a much expanded GATT with real coercive teeth. Central to the founding of the WTO were the twin drives of managing the trade rivalry among the leading industrial countries while containing the threat posed by the South to the prevailing global economic structure. In this sense, the WTO must be seen as a continuation or extension of the same Northern reaction that drove

**UN Conference on Trade and Development (UNCTAD)**

UNCTAD's first Secretary General, Argentine Raul Prebisch, had noted structural obstacles to the South's development, especially deteriorating term of trade with the North. To rectify these imbalances, Prebisch suggested more aid, preferential tariffs, stable commodity prices and import-substitution, none of which were acceptable to the North. 'The Northern offensive escalated during UNCTAD VIII, held in Cartagena (Colombia), in 1992. At this watershed meeting, the North successfully opposed all linkages of UNCTAD discussions with the Uruguay Round negotiations of the GATT and managed to erode UNCTAD's negotiation functions, thus calling its existence into question. UNCTAD's main function would henceforth be limited to 'analysis, consensus building on some trade-related issues, and technical assistance...[Some analysts say]s that UNCTAD has been made obsolete by the creation of the WTO' (Bello, 1999).

structural adjustment. Indeed, the WTO.... represents the defeat of everything that the South fought for in UNCTAD....The WTO institutionalises free trade, the most favoured nation principle, and national treatment, as the pillars of the new world trading order. National treatment....is perhaps the most revolutionary of these principles and the most threatening to the South for it gives foreign service providers, from telecommunications companies to lawyers to educational agencies, the same rights and privileges as their domestic counterparts' (Bello, 1999).

Pre-existing trade agreements, such as Mercosur (Brazil, Argentina, Uruguay, Paraguay), NAFTA (Canada, Mexico, US), CARICOM (Caribbean) and the Central America Common Market in Latin America and the Caribbean, do have special rights under the WTO (see Free Trade Area of the Americas (FTAA) below).

The anti-South thrust of the WTO is even more evident in the Agreement on Trade-Related Investment Measures (TRIMs) and the Agreement on Trade-Related Intellectual Property Rights (TRIPs). TRIMs do not allow (developing) countries to require that a certain amount of the raw materials used in their industrial production be from local resources. Similarly, TRIPs allow the more 'advanced' North (especially the US) to protect its technological inventions and patents. The double insult, however, is that TRIPs 'has opened the way for the (Northern) privatisation of products developed from genetic processes or communal technological innovation in the South.... [This had led to what] some scholars in the South have labeled 'biopiracy' (Ibid).

Southern countries show up other hypocrisies in the WTO, which 'while it pushes for free trade on the South, in some of its subsidiary agreements it actually promotes monopoly for the North in others. This is true... of the Agreement on Agriculture (AOA)...Prior to the GATT's Uruguay Round (1986-94), agriculture was de facto outside GATT discipline, mainly because the US had sought in the 1950s a waiver...which prohibited quantitative restrictions on imports...Later Europe entered the fray and one effect of these moves was the transformation of the EU from being a net food importer into a net food exporter in the 1970s. By the beginning of the Uruguay Round in the mid-eighties, the EU's Common Agricultural Policy (CAP) had developed into ... a complex web of price and sales guarantees, subsidies, and other support measures that largely insulated (European) farmers' incomes from market forces...' The competition between the agricultural superpowers turned fierce, but it was not so much their subsidised farmers who suffered. The victims were largely farmers in the South....The EU and US gradually came to realise that continuing along the same path could only lead to a no-win situation for both...This mutual realisation of the need for rules in the struggle for Third World country markets is what led to the EU and US to press for inclusion of agriculture in the Uruguay Round....The two superpowers resorted to the rhetoric of free trade to regulate a condition of monopolistic competition....Subsidised Northern producers who make a mockery of global free trade in agriculture fight for developing country markets, squeezing the non-subsidised farmers in the (South)...'

There are other inequalities built into the WTO system...Decision making is perhaps among the most blatant...While pro-WTO propaganda has projected that agency as a one nation/one vote organisation...in fact, it is quite undemocratic...While at the (World) Bank and the IMF, the prime mechanism of control is the size of rich countries' capital subscriptions...at the WTO, Northern domination is achieved via what is euphemistically referred to as 'consensus' ...which is managed by four countries, the Quads: the US, Japan, the EU and Canada...Indeed, so undemocratic is the WTO that decisions are arrived at informally, via caucuses convoked in the corridors ...by the big trading powers. The formal sessions are reserved for speeches...' (Ibid).

The 1999 Third Ministerial WTO meeting in Seattle has revealed many of these flaws to a wider public. With an estimated 40,000 international NGO, labour, environmental and other protesters outside, the opening session was cancelled. Days later, the meeting came to an end with no new Millennium Round in sight, as internal discord equalled the din from civil society protesters. This has been heralded as the largest protest in the US since 1968 (at the height of the Vietnam war) and perhaps the most significant demonstration ever against a multilateral institution. External protesters decried the current globalised, Northern controlled economic order overall and the lack of transparency of the WTO. Internal debates focused on:

- North vs. South on globalisation/WTO – Southern countries felt they were abused in previous trade talks, having agreed to open their economies to Northern exports in return for promises that were never fulfilled. The South wanted to review previous WTO agreements before initiating discussion on new issues such as investment. The EU wanted to press forward and the US refused to review old accords.
- The US vs. Europe on agriculture – The US, backed by other large agro-exporters such as Brazil and Argentina, wanted Europe to open its markets and reduce its subsidies to farmers. The EU agreed to limited reforms over time.
- US vs. the South on labour/environmental standards – The US wanted to include these as WTO issues. The South felt this was in large part the US wanting to protect its own industries and a Democratic partisan ploy to gain support in the upcoming US presidential elections, rather than a genuine desire to help labour and the environment in the South (e.g. there was no reference to either of these concerns in the recent bilateral US/China trade deal).

Other issues which ricocheted off the halls of the meeting were the lack of transparency, democracy and general shambles the WTO is in. The anger of the Southern delegates at being sidelined was palpable. Even the US and EU admitted at the conference's closing event that major changes needed to take place. 'As long as there exist no conditions of transparency, openness and participation which permit a balanced outcome in the interest of all members of the WTO we will not reach the necessary ministerial level of consensus which this conference requires,' read an open letter to the press from all participating Latin American/Caribbean countries except Argentina, Brazil and Mexico. The so called Millennium Round did not go forward on time. A special session was held in Geneva in December 1999 and another in January 2000 to evaluate the future of the organisation. After the debacle in Seattle, the future of the WTO stands at a crossroads.

## Membership of the WTO

At the time of the Seattle Ministerial Meeting in late November 1999, the WTO had 134 member nations, 80% from the South. Thirty more Southern countries, including China, had applied for membership to be approved in Seattle, but China among others suspended negotiations in the light of the Seattle controversies.

## Mexico: fallout from the 'battle of Seattle'

(Edited from Ross, 1999)

Protests at the World Trade Organisation meeting had repercussions in Latin America.

On the eve of the battle of Seattle, the startling street protests in that US city against the World Trade Organisation (WTO) and the impact of neo-liberal globalisation, 200 horsemen galloped up to the doors of the Mexican Senate and demanded an audience with Commerce Secretary Herminio Blanco. Denied admittance, the members of El Barzón, a union of farmers and small-business owners frustrated by their unpayable bank loans, dismounted, tied their steeds to the Senate gate and set fire to bales of cotton in the street. The farmers, who are particularly concerned about a flood of cheap US cotton, meat and apples which they say displaces their home grown products from the Mexican marketplace, had been on the road for two months, riding in from Ciudad Juárez on the US border, over mountains and across deserts. 'There goes your free trade!' bellowed one rider as the nervous horses all but buried the Senate steps in steaming horse dung.

The next day, 30 November 1999, Blanco was in Seattle, heading the Mexican delegation of the WTO's Millennium Round of trade talks meant to set the agenda for world trade into the next century. Also on hand were thousands of protesters, including small farmers, workers, indigenous groups, anarchists and pensioners, during four days of some of the largest public protests ever seen in the US.

Delegates complained to the press: 'We can't let (labour and environmental) issues contaminate the free trade agenda,' Blanco said.

'Mano dura (heavy hand) in Seattle!' Mexican headlines cried in language usually reserved for military dictatorships. On December 11, protesters and striking students from Mexico's National Autonomous University (UNAM), retaliated against police treatment of marchers in Seattle by stoning the US Embassy in Mexico City in the most violent demonstration against the fortress-like facility in recent memory.

The Seattle meeting adjourned without agreement on an agenda, let alone the start of trade talks. The marchers' global message, calling for solidarity among diverse causes to confront the impact of free trade on the world's workers and marginalised peoples, was decried by Latin American and other delegates as a conspiracy to protect US and European interests. Brazilian President Fernando Henrique Cardoso said his country 'made it clear that the multilateral trade system has to choose between two alternatives: a regime that protects the rich and hurts the poor, or a universal system that also gives just access to markets for less-developed countries.'

Mexican President Ernesto Zedillo, an outspoken champion of free trade, said 'it would be a tragic step backward for the liberalisation of world wide commerce if the protesters' issues were accepted by the WTO...' Nonetheless, Mexico has often given in to such human and environmental rights regulations in order to consummate commercial treaties. Labour and environmental side agreements, criticised as largely ornamental, were attached to the North American Free Trade Agreement (NAFTA) at US insistence, and the recently inked free trade pact with the European Union requires compliance with international human rights norms, issues the Mexican government considers illicit protectionism.

Latin America's own anti-globalisation movements welcomed the events in Seattle. In Mexico, the battle against globalisation has been given a boost by the largely Mayan Zapatista Army of National Liberation (EZLN), which rose up in arms on 1 January 1994, just as NAFTA came into being. In 1999, their third international 'Encounter in Defence of Humanity and Against Neoliberalism' took place in Belém, Brazil, and brought together 3,000 trade unionists, environmentalists and indigenous representatives.

## Free Trade Area of the Americas (FTAA)

Particular to the Western Hemisphere is the FTAA, set to begin operating in 2005. Parallel to its ongoing development, the Business Forum of the Americas (consisting of transnational corporate interests) maintains its insistence on a treaty based on the principle of 'national treatment' which would require governments to give foreign investors the same treatment they offer to domestic enterprises. Whereas national treatment under GATT only applied to taxes and regulations on imported goods, the Business Forum would have this expanded under the FTAA to include vast areas of domestic economic activity previously exempt, such as granting of natural resource permits, licensing for health and social services, concessions to electric and water supplies, communications, and many more. Moreover, FTAA should 'extend uniform, non-discriminatory national treatment to capital originating from outside the FTAA... Investors from Europe and Asia would receive the same treatment as investors from within the Americas.'

The Business Forum has also called for restrictions on 'performance requirements,' or conditions on investment that governments use to hold investors accountable to domestic policies. However, governments should have the right to impose performance requirements on foreign investors and treat local, family and community businesses and publicly owned enterprises more favourably than foreign ones.

'The weakness of the regulatory frameworks for economic activities in many areas dominated by foreign investment have time and again been laid bare with respect to safeguards of national sovereignty; consumers' rights; competition policies; workers' rights; women's rights; children's rights; indigenous peoples' rights; environmental and health standards. The regression in institutional frameworks in the majority of Latin American countries is not just a sign of a new historical phenomenon but also a consequence of accepting the fallacy that foreign investment is good in and of itself and must be promoted without restriction' (Dillon, 1998).

In 1999, the InterAmerican Development Bank (IDB) announced it would provide US$50 million to help countries in the region prepare for the start of FTAA in 2005.

## In Focus: Free Trade Area of the Americas

(Edited from Karen Hansen-Kuhn, 1998)

In April 1998 the leaders of 34 Western Hemisphere countries gathered in Santiago, Chile, for the Second Summit of the Americas. Economic integration issues dominated the meeting. The Summit's final declaration promised to create an historic Free Trade Area of the Americas (FTAA) linking all of the hemisphere's economies (except Cuba's) by the year 2005.

During the first Summit, (Miami 1994), Mexico was held out as the model of economic reform and NAFTA as the model trade agreement. Just ten days later, however, the Mexican peso underwent a massive devaluation. That, coupled with the austerity conditions attached to the bailout package by the US Treasury and the IMF, sent the Mexican economy into a deep depression and reduced the purchasing power of Mexican wages and the prices of export goods. Mexico's currency crisis and the financial crisis in East Asia rocked stock markets around the world.

While these economic crises dampened US public and congressional enthusiasm for free-trade agreements, governments continued the process set in motion at the Summit. At their March 1998 meeting in Costa Rica, the hemisphere's trade ministers' final declaration called for 'considerable progress' toward an FTAA by the year 2000. Over the past few years, numerous trade and investment agreements have been signed by different countries in Latin America and the Caribbean. In addition to regional pacts, such as NAFTA, Mercosur, the Andean Pact, and the Caribbean Community (Caricom), there are bilateral agreements, such as the one between Chile and Mexico, as well as accords between regional groupings and individual countries.

In the process of establishing a Free Trade Area of the Americas, it is likely that the Mercosur countries (Brazil, Argentina, Paraguay, and Uruguay, along with associate members Chile and Bolivia) will negotiate as a group, as will the Andean Pact, while the United States, Canada, and Mexico are expected to negotiate as individual countries. If the non-NAFTA countries in the hemisphere do join together, co-ordinating their negotiating strategies and building on existing trading blocs, they would have greater leverage in their negotiations with the NAFTA countries than if they were to negotiate as individual countries. By acting in concert through Mercosur and other groups in negotiations with the Asia-Pacific Economic Co-operation (APEC) countries, and particularly with the European Union, these countries have enhanced their leverage all the more in negotiations with the US.

Because of their size and economic power, NAFTA and Mercosur will likely serve as the two principal models for agreements reached during the FTAA negotiations. Despite their apparent differences, NAFTA is a trade agreement and Mercosur is a common market, they are rather similar accords, as both entail extensive liberalisation of trade and investment regimes. NAFTA establishes a free-trade area, in which barriers to trade in goods produced in the member countries are removed but each country retains the ability to set tariffs on goods from non-member countries. However, NAFTA is more than a mere trade agreement; it also includes measures to liberalise capital flows, protect intellectual property rights, open new sectors to foreign investment, and facilitate temporary labour mobility of certain classes of businesspeople and professionals.

Both NAFTA and Mercosur include measures to deregulate foreign investment. Each provides that foreign investors (with some exceptions) from member countries be treated no differently than local investors. Both agreements also prohibit the application of performance requirements that obligate investors to achieve a certain level of exports or technology transfer. NAFTA goes so far as to prohibit performance requirements on any foreign investments, even those from non-member countries.

These provisions, along with others on public and financial services, have the effect of locking in the structural adjustment programs implemented in the region over the past decade. Thus, both NAFTA and Mercosur have serious negative implications for member countries. If countries cannot regulate foreign investment, for example, they will be unable to implement co-ordinated industrial or developmental strategies. They will be forced to continue to reduce wages, to allow poor working conditions, and to ignore environmental regulations in increasingly desperate moves to attract mobile international capital.

47

Evidence of the failure of the NAFTA model of economic integration continues to mount. In the aftermath of the Mexican peso crisis, the IMF and the US Treasury insisted that Mexico maintain its commitments under NAFTA by continuing to liberalise trade and investment regimes and by maintaining high interest rates in order to shore up the peso. Higher interest rates, decreased purchasing power of consumers, and increased competition with imported goods have had a devastating impact on small and medium-scale producers and retail businesses. Additionally, some two million Mexicans have lost their jobs, and though such macro-economic indicators as GDP growth have turned positive in the last few years, the standard of living of most Mexicans has deteriorated. The number of Mexicans pushed into the informal sector and working for less than the minimum wage, without benefits, or less than full time has increased dramatically, while the purchasing power of the basic minimum wage has dropped by 24%.

The negative impacts of Mercosur on its members are not as evident because many of the trade liberalisation measures only began to be phased in recently. But some signs of troubling fallout already appeared. Union federations in Brazil, Argentina, Paraguay, and Uruguay have held massive demonstrations during Mercosur summit meetings to protest growing unemployment. Meanwhile, already strapped governments in the region have found themselves competing with each other to offer the greatest tax incentives to investors attracted to the Mercosur market.

There is little evidence that the NAFTA/Mercosur model would establish a solid foundation for economic relationships that foster sustainable development and economic progress in member countries. The NAFTA experience has demonstrated that the benefits of trade will not automatically trickle down to the population as a whole. Instead, trade agreements must be specifically designed to serve as tools for development that benefits everyone, not just those at the top. A critical first step in achieving a different kind of trade agreement in the Americas is to open the process to a broader representation of different social sectors. Labour, environmental, and other relevant social sectors should be included in the negotiation process. The resulting agreements should affirm such internationally recognised accords as the International Labour Organisation Conventions, the UN Convention to Eliminate All Forms of Discrimination Against Women, and the Inter-American Convention on Human Rights. Additionally, any consensus reached on these issues must be included within the text of the trade agreements, not in unenforceable side agreements.

The approach to investment policy should also be changed to balance the needs of foreign investors for clear rules with the needs of the national economy. Governments should retain the right to impose performance requirements on foreign investors, as well as the right to protect small and medium-scale producers and other key economic sectors in order to pursue national development plans. Countries' rights to maintain food and nutritional security (for example, by excluding basic grains from trade liberalisation measures) should also be established.

## Alliance for Responsible Trade: a manifesto

(Excerpted from Alliance for Responsible Trade, 1999)

This statement highlights major points from *Alternatives for the Americas*, that outlines concrete and viable alternatives to the Free Trade Area of the Americas (FTAA) based on the interests of the peoples of our hemisphere.

GOAL

Integration needs to shift from an emphasis on exports based on the exploitation of natural resources and workers to sustainable economic activity that roots capital locally and nationally and promotes human rights. An alternative approach to hemispheric integration should be based on the following pillars:

1. Give the People a Voice – We support the development of a democratic and accountable process for negotiating trade and investment agreements in the United States and throughout the hemisphere. Such a process must replace the current control of the economic integration agenda by major corporations and the US Executive Branch (through fast-track authority).

2. Strengthen Environmental Standards and Labour Rights Protections for all – The enforcement of core labour and environmental rights and standards should be at the centre of any new agreements. Labour rights protections must extend to all workers, regardless of their immigration status, gender, or race. Experience around the world demonstrates that these standards will not be protected if they are left to market forces or relegated to unenforceable 'side agreements.'

3. Shift Finance from Speculation to Long-term Investment in Productive Activities – Governments should be encouraged to adopt new local, national and global rules to discourage harmful speculative activity, including speculation on currencies, and to encourage lasting investments in productive and sustainable local economic activities.

4. Close the Gap Between and Within Rich and Poor Countries – While the European integration process included the establishment of massive structural funds and labour mobility to equalise conditions among the member countries, debt reduction measures might be more relevant in this hemisphere.

49

5. Ensure Food Security and the Right to Development Planning – Access for foreign products and investments should be negotiated with due concern for national development plans and priorities. Protection of critical sectors, such as food production, must be the right of each country so as to ensure the rights and well being of all people.

## The death of development?

(Edited from Jordan, 1999)

The World Bank, as the largest international development institution, has a special responsibility not only to help developing countries choose appropriate development paths but also to protect the right of countries to develop in ways that they themselves see as appropriate. Rhetorically at least the Bank has embraced this and the responsibility to alleviate poverty. The international trade framework has already limited the range of development options available to developing countries and the amount of time available to developing countries in which they can get their national policies in tune with international market demands. The World Bank has not sounded the alarm bells in response to these and other problems created for developing countries in the WTO regime. Instead, the World Bank appears to have chosen to adjust its concept of 'development' to accommodate the existing international trade regime, even though some of its own staff argue that trade agreements have not taken into account the reality in developing countries. The World Bank should reconsider the parameters of its alliance with the WTO to argue for trade agreements that better take into account development.

There is ample evidence that the economy of the 21$^{st}$ century will be a global economy largely driven by private capital flows. Private finance and investment is the most important factor in economic globalisation. Private financial flows account for 1.9 trillion US dollars a day. Public expenditure for development have decreased by 22 percent in real terms since 1990, while private capital flows to developing countries have soared by more than 500 percent.

There are troublesome consequences that arise from a global economy that are not well addressed through the World Bank and the WTO. Expansion of market economies, trade liberalisation, export-driven development and privatisation may have contributed to growth but have had negative consequences as well. Economic globalisation in its current form has resulted in a concentration of wealth within the rich industrialised countries and growing environmental degradation caused by primary resource extraction in the poor countries. Gaps between rich and poor both nationally and globally continue to grow (World Development Report 1999). National economic destabilisation is a more frequent phenomenon within the globalised economy and is especially hard-hitting in developing countries. On the latter issue, rapid changes in the availability of private capital are largely responsible for the current instability in Asia, Russia and Brazil. Developing nations that have responded to pressure to liberalise their national economies have suffered greatly in the last two years from overexposure to international investors. Weak regulatory structures and market failures combined with nervous international investors have in effect created a situation where there are now millions of newly poor people in developing countries.

The development paradigm underpinning the World Bank is predicated on the assumption that economic growth will alleviate poverty. For over two decades the preferred pattern of economic growth has been through facilitating developing countries to participate in the global market place. The World Bank has emphasised exports and policies that attract international capital. The Bank's macro-economic policy advice is predicated on the assumption that the policies should facilitate expanding trade and investment. Critics have attacked this model for almost as long as it has existed because of its impact on the poor. Midway through the 1990s the World Bank tacitly admitted that negative social impacts were resulting from policy conditions placed upon developing countries.

An emerging convergence between the World Bank and the WTO is likely to end fledgling attempts to define the development paradigm through a social lens. The convergence of the world's premier development institution with the WTO could spell the death of development, though not the end of poverty. There are three major reasons for this. First, some of the current trade agreements fundamentally misdiagnose development problems and therefore impose heavy burdens on developing countries. Second, the enforcement mechanism at the WTO can reinforce liberalisation in a way that the World Bank has never been able to do. Furthermore, the enforcement mechanism presents a real threat to democratic due process in developing countries and can limit the development options of very small and poor countries. Third, trade agreements place a burden of adjustment on those countries not able to represent their own interests when the agreements were formulated. The convergence between the WTO and the World Bank indicate that the Bank is already making a choice to reinforce a singular approach to growth. It is also relegating itself to a secondary position in the global public policy arena as an institution that no longer makes decisions but can only address the consequences of decisions taken elsewhere.

In documents prepared for its Board, the World Bank recognises that the WTO has done very little to build developing country ownership of the new trade regimes. There is also subtle evidence that the World Bank recognises that some trade rules are not necessarily beneficial to developing countries. In a paper prepared for the World Bank's Committee of the Whole the World Bank notes that trade reforms require approaches that focus on the development needs of poorer countries if they are to have a development payoff. The World Bank argues that the required approaches would differ considerably from those approaches now embraced by the WTO that simply duplicate practices in industrial countries.

One of the most important elements of the World Bank's involvement in trade is the Integrated Framework which augments the capacity of developing countries to use trade as a vehicle for development. The Integrated Framework was initiated by the 1996 WTO Ministerial Declaration for a Plan of Action and launched in 1997 in Geneva. It has two official objectives: to enable least developed countries to use trade as an effective vehicle for development and to effectively advance their interests through the WTO. Staff at the World Bank describe the Integrated Framework in the following ways: a tool through which developing countries can increase their capacity to make trade rules useful; a mechanism through which the World Bank can help the WTO generate a broader sense of local ownership over the new trade rules within developing countries. The Integrated Framework operates as a joint program between the World Bank, the WTO, the International Monetary Fund, UNDP, and the United Nations Committee on Trade and Development to provide an integrated framework of trade related assistance. This could also be understood to mean providing assistance in an efficient manner, i.e. one that avoids duplication. Forty developing countries have undertaken trade related needs assessments, the first step in joining the Integrated Framework. While the Integrated Framework provides the background for integrating trade into development, the implementation of trade rules is actually done at the project level. It is here at the operational level that trade can break out of the poverty alleviation framework. Policy-based lending rarely mentions trade rules or trade reform as a goal. However, loans often are predicated on the same objectives as those underscored by trade rules. According to the World Bank's own accounting, between 1981 and 1994 it made 238 loans that supported liberalisation of trade or foreign exchange policy to 75 different countries. Since 1995, 54 additional IBRD and IDA adjustment operations (65% of all adjustment operations) have supported exchange rate and trade policy reform.

Ecuador provides an example of how this process actually works. Ecuador joined the WTO in 1996 and in the process of accession agreed to reduce or eliminate a number of trade barriers. The World Bank, immediately upon Ecuador's accession, began to negotiate and create conditions for US$21 million woth of trade investment. The private sector exporters in Ecuador have matched the Bank's investment with US$21 million bringing the total project budget to US$42.6. Through the process of negotiating the loan the Ecuadorian government had to adopt a number of new laws and as a condition must in the future rewrite regulations. The loan itself was conditioned upon the passage of a new Foreign Trade and Investment Law. Key provisions in this law are:

• The creation of a Foreign Trade and Investment Council that formulates and implements trade policies and regulations on a whole host of issues. The Council is made up of ministers and the Presidents of the federations of chambers of exporters, industry, agriculture and commerce. Labour and consumer groups do not have a seat at this table.

• Consolidation of public authority within one institution for trade policy making and execution.

• Decentralisation of support services for businesses and privatisation for profit making activities.

The project demonstrates how policy agendas can converge between the Bank and the WTO. The ultimate impact on Ecuador is yet to be seen. However, what we do know is that large segments of the law in Ecuador have or will change in order to create a friendlier export-driven environment for business. These laws were formulated without input from labour representatives. Labour is likely to be one of the first constituents impacted by the privatisation components of the project and by the national foreign export board. Similarly, consumers' groups were not represented in the participatory process. The codification of what are essentially voluntary standards to replace national compulsory quality standards calls into question the purpose of the standards. Lastly, the lack of a national regulatory structure is far from ideal.

As noted earlier, there are three major problems stemming from the convergence of the WTO and the World Bank. First, some of the current trade agreements fundamentally misdiagnose development problems. Second, the enforcement mechanism at the WTO can reinforce liberalisation in a way the World Bank has never been able to do. Furthermore, the enforcement mechanism presents a real threat to democratic due process in developing countries and can limit the development options of very small and poor countries. Third, trade agreements place a burden of adjustment on those countries not able to represent their own interests when the agreements were formulated. The World Bank seems to have chosen to help mitigate the impacts of the trade regime on its borrowers instead of reshaping the rules of negotiation and defending the right to develop.

The trends reinforced by the WTO will have profound consequences for developing countries, development and the World Bank. Development specialists argue that the development budget is now being committed by political negotiations at the trade level. Implementation is likely to be financed by the World Bank as it has been in Ecuador but never treated as a development decision.

Another example of the narrowing options for development paths is the erosion of trade preferences in agreements like Lomé. The Lomé agreement establishes a preferential customs system and trade guarantees for countries, among others, [in the Caribbean] trading with the European Union. The recent ruling on bananas in the WTO outlawed preferential treatment in the Lomé agreement for small-scale banana producers in the Caribbean. Small-scale banana producers will now have to compete with Dole, United Fruit and other US-based companies for access to the European markets. Terms of trade and national incomes will weaken for developing countries as Lomé-like preferential trade agreements with development objectives at their core are phased out. The negative impact in small states like those in the Caribbean is expected to be especially disruptive and will require what the World Bank calls 'innovative approaches.' Those approaches have yet to be identified by the World Bank, the EU or the WTO. Most of the trade agreements suggest a possibility for alternatives but do not provide a process for developing countries to pursue alternatives.

Globalisation and specifically trade agreements as currently negotiated and implemented are expected to have a negative impact on most developing countries but in particular on small states and the least developed countries. For small states, the loss of preferential access to large markets (as described above through the Lomé Agreement) and declines in aid resources in the face of evolving world trade arrangements and rules imply a significant adverse social impact and a negative impact on incomes. Some of these states are left in a condition of neither aid nor trade. The solution to declining aid and trade options identified by the World Bank is more aid and more time for adjustment. The latter however, is not possible with the new enforcement mechanism and the former is only possible if there is considerable political will amongst donor countries. The historical trend in lower aid flows underscores the need for other solutions.

As the policy agendas between the World Bank and the WTO converge, observers ask two key questions: what is development and what will it become in the future? In materials produced for the Board of the World Bank, the Bank appears to be using trade and development as interchangeable concepts.

54

Acknowledging that trade has expanded into a complex and subtle web of issues that form the crux of the development agenda is central to understanding the role of the Bank. The Bank now seems to consider trade to be at the centre of the development paradigm. A representative from the Haiti government challenged the World Bank on this very issue when he said that he had been trying to understand how trade could serve as a vehicle for development. As far as he understood, it could well be the other way around: development could be the vehicle for trade. If World Bank lending operations continue to follow the trade agreements, by default the development agenda will be displaced. The World Bank will end up mitigating impacts, cleaning up messes and lending for social safety nets instead of helping countries choose and implement development paths that address the social and economic needs of the country in question. All of the work now undertaken to practice a participatory, borrower-driven development agenda will be lost to the process of adjusting to a new trade regime. In other words, we could be witnessing the death of a development paradigm that embeds liberalism within a social, poverty reduction oriented framework.

Even though the World Bank admits that trade agreements are harsh on the economies of developing countries, it has thus far not been prepared to argue for special rights, a more transparent process within the WTO, or for reviewing existing agreements to determine their impact on development options. All evidence points to the World Bank developing an agreement with the WTO that will facilitate raw private capital flows without intra-or-inter country social consequences diagnosed or even the interests of developing countries at the forefront.

The nuts and bolts of the World Bank's current relationship with the WTO suggest that the World Bank is enthusiastic about the existing trade agreements and will play its part in their implementation. The World Bank seems to gloss over the warnings produced by its own staff in its enthusiasm to embrace trade liberalisation as defined through the WTO. The impact on smaller economies, greater volatility in the global market place and the enormous costs associated with integration and implementation of trade rules could easily derail development agendas and leave developing countries more dependent upon World Bank assistance. Adjustment operations will continue to dominate the development agenda but will now have an extra dimension of adjusting to the new trade rules. While its own future as a lending institution is secured when globalisation results in rules that keep developing countries at a permanent disadvantage, its ability to solidify a new development paradigm that embeds liberalism in a social framework will be lost. Furthermore, it will not reach its stated goal of poverty alleviation.

As one World Bank staff person noted off the record, 'if you want to keep these countries poor, implement the WTO.'

## International capital flows unleashed

(Edited from Green, 1999)

The chaos in global capital markets since the mid-1990s has had a profound impact on the world's poor. Beginning with the Mexican crash of 1994, what Michel Camdessus, the then IMF Managing Director, prophetically described at the time as 'the first major crisis of our new world of globalised financial markets' has swept across East Asia and Russia, before returning to batter Brazil and other parts of Latin America (private financial flows to the region dropped from US$105 billion in 1997 to US$85 billion in 1998 and are predicted to be as low as US$60 billion in 1999).

### UNCTAD

UNCTAD predicted a 1% contraction in Latin America's GDP, as a remaining effect of the Asian crisis. ECLAC admits that the international financial crisis has taken a much heavier toll on the region, especially South America, than originally expected. In the South, the crisis has led to a slump in trade, rise in the cost of credit and decreased investment, UNCTAD added. Commodity prices have fallen by an average of 13% in 1999, compounding 1998's 12% drop. Trade within MERCOSUR shrank 30% during the international crisis. In capital investments, it has been 'flight to quality,' as investors purchased US Treasury bonds. 72% of direct foreign investment that reached the South in 1998 went toward purchasing existing assets, mainly privatised public enterprises, rather than creating new productive capacity.

The crisis has been precipitated by sudden capital outflows. The globalised economy, particularly in developing countries, now suffers from heightened and endemic instability, punctuated by frequent currency crises, systemic bank collapses and a disturbing loss of control by governments over their countries' economic destinies.

The financial crisis of 1997/8 is deemed to be over. A year and a half after Russia's August 1998 default on its domestic debt obligations, the mood has swung back to excessive euphoria, on the strength of market rebounds in most of the affected countries. But there is a continuing downward spiral of unemployment, falling wages, and social dislocation which endures long after macro-economic recovery is under way.

The extraordinary rise of global financial flows has been the single most important economic development in the last quarter of the 20th century.

The breakdown in the early 1970s of the global system of fixed exchange rates established at the Bretton Woods Conference unleashed a series of booms – foreign exchange markets in the 1970s, bond markets in the 1980s, and global equity markets in the 1990s. Each boom was facilitated by technological innovation, especially in computerisation, and the removal of barriers to capital flows.

By April 1998, global daily turnover on the foreign exchange market came to $1.5 trillion. This figure had risen 26% since 1995, which was in turn 45% higher than in 1992 and continues to double every seven years. Moreover, total world government foreign reserves are $1.6 trillion, about one day's worth of market capital. Since global trade currently accounts for about $5.4 trillion per year, capital flows are one hundred times as great as trade flows. In the light of such disparity, there is little doubt that a large proportion of capital flows bears little direct relation to trade and investment. Most are speculative, an attempt to earn profits by anticipating correctly how different countries' exchange rates will move. Analysts say the amount of exchange market activity linked to the 'real' economy, is no more than 10%. Total net private flows to emerging markets from 1990-98 were estimated at $1.25 trillion, compared to net official flows of just $210 billion.

These investment flows consisted of a combination of direct investment, portfolio investment in stocks and bonds, and loans from commercial banks. Over the 1990-98 period, net flows in these different categories fluctuated enormously, particularly bank lending. The financial crisis of 1997/8 led to an abrupt exit by international banks from emerging markets. The increase in financial flows has been accompanied by an increase in volatility, out of which there are large profits to be made.

Technological developments, particularly in information technology, facilitated the rise of the financial markets, as did the rising volume of capital controlled by institutional investors such as pension and mutual funds. But policy makers also played a crucial role with the combination of domestic financial deregulation and capital account liberalisation (allowing domestic borrowers and lenders to gain access to the international market, and foreign investors to enter hitherto protected parts of the domestic economy).

The World Bank's structural adjustment programmes, so-called 'Mission Creep' at the IMF, as well as bilateral and regional trade agreements and investment treaties have all contributed to unbridled financial flows. Conventional wisdom has it that financial liberalisation leads to growth which in turn leads to poverty reduction and development.

The IMF and Bank continue to advocate for a new paradigm of capital flows which implies limiting the role of the public sector (including the Bank and Fund themselves – in early 2000, the IMF did concede that some capital flow controls might be beneficial in certain limited cases). The Bretton Woods Institutions are promoting this through:

- SAPs (structural adjustment programmes)
- direct private sector support through World Bank bodies
- CAL (capital account liberalisation)
- HIPC and
- promotion of these ideas through high profile public events and statements.

The focus on increased private financial flows has coincided with a decline in official aid grants and loans.

However, the head of the UN's Economic Commission for Latin America and the Caribbean, notes that 'there is no evidence of an association between capital account liberalisation and economic growth, and some in the opposite direction.' In April 1999, the World Bank Vice-President for Latin America and the Caribbean told reporters, 'My belief is that we should stop talking about crises and start talking about extreme volatility. Essentially, I think we should be preparing ourselves for a perpetual state of volatility rather than a recurring crisis.'

In order to defend their currencies against international raiders, governments are forced to assemble large war chests of hard currency reserves. For emerging markets as a whole, over half the $1.25 trillion private inflows from 1990-98 went to build up foreign reserves, money that cannot be spent on health, education and other social needs. Moreover, competition for investment among countries is great. As foreign direct investment (FDI) becomes more important as a source of financing, there is increasing incentive for developing countries to open their doors with a welcoming smile to FDI. This is achieved with policies such as:

- tax concessions to TNIs, which reduces government revenues
- easing restrictions on profit remittances, which can result in less domestic investment and make capital flows more volatile
- relaxing restrictions on foreign ownership of national enterprises
- easing restrictions on expatriate work laws and strengthening foreign patent protection
- removing labour bargaining rights (Woodward, 1998).

Lower growth, increased volatility, rising inequality and falling government spending –financial deregulation has obvious negative impacts on the poor. Although such impacts were made salient by the impact of the currency crises that afflicted Asia from 1997-98 , the important point is that financial deregulation can be harmful for human development, even when spectacular crashes do not occur.

There is growing acceptance that the breakneck and forced pace of liberalisation has created a world in which economies are increasingly vulnerable to crisis. The IMF Research Department points out the empirical link, noting that 'crises had struck six of the ten largest recipients of private market financing in the 1990s.' These are Mexico, Korea, Brazil, Thailand, Indonesia and Russia – the others are Hong Kong, Argentina, China and Turkey.

The process was not simply a response to policies being imposed from the outside. Powerful financial and business lobbies in Korea and the other Asian economies also pursued deregulation, intent on securing access to cheap capital. The tragedy is that the Asian tiger economies, which boasted some of the highest levels of domestic savings rates in the world, had no need for short-term capital flows from abroad.

Banking crises have also become a feature of the new globalised finance markets. The past 20 years have seen more than 90 serious banking crises, each of which resulted in bank losses that, in proportion to GDP, exceeded the costs of America's banking collapse during the Great Depression. Bank crashes invariably have to be bailed out by governments, leaving a legacy of increased public debt, and a burden on state spending which can last for decades. The extraordinary cost and depth of the banking crisis has led to a great emphasis on financial sector reform in the West. The response has been along the lines of enabling the banking system to cope with open capital markets. Far less consideration has been given to whether capital account liberalisation should have happened in the first place, and the arguments for reversing this process in the wake of the crisis.

Financial liberalisation may indeed be anti-poor in normal times, but the most devastating impact occurs when it helps precipitate a financial crisis of the kind seen in numerous Southern countries in the second half of the 1990s. Massive job losses, reduced working hours, falling wages and the shift to worse-paying work have severely reduced income in the crisis-hit countries. Women have borne the brunt of the crisis in a number of different ways. Light manufacturing sectors such as textiles and garments, where women usually make up a large majority of the workforce, have been badly hit by the recession and banking crisis. Wages are falling due to the switch to temporary jobs, and there are no entitlements to benefits. In their traditional role as family caretakers, women have to pick up the pieces left by the decline in state services, for example by looking after sick children and relatives. Finally, there is widespread evidence of family breakdown and an increase in domestic violence as a result of the (Asian) crash.

In its most recent overview of the social impact of the crisis, the World Bank saw some grounds for hoping that by mid-1999 the worst was over and drew three main conclusions from the traumas of 1997-99:
- The social impact of the crisis was swift, deep and very complex
- Government and civil society responses helped to limit irreversible hardship in important areas
- Setbacks to long-term social programmes were substantial and a renewed focus on social strategy and reform was needed.

But the Bank admitted that 'the social crisis is still unfolding.' People do not bounce back as easily as macro-economic indicators. Moreover, countries have emerged from their crises burdened by significantly larger public debts and increased levels of foreign ownership of their economies.

Although the G-7 governments and international organisations such as the World Bank and the regional development banks (African, Asian and Inter-American Development Banks) have all been involved in responding to the crisis, the key policy role has been played by the IMF. The IMF is also central to discussions over the reform of the International Financial Architecture.

The Fund's general approach has been to deal with each crash country on a case by case basis, much as it did in the debt crises of the 1980s. In Asia, the IMF's response was based on its analysis that the causes of the crisis were domestic economic failings. No blame was attached to the international financial system. The IMF at no point questioned the wisdom of the Asian governments' decision (backed by the IFIs) to open up their capital markets in the first place. From its experience in Latin America and Africa it took a predilection for austerity, while from its reforms in the transition economies in Eastern Europe, it has brought a far more detailed and all-embracing approach to conditionality and widespread privatisation.

The IMF's handling of the Asian crash has prompted a greater wave of criticism, from a broader group of people and institutions, than at any previous time in its 55-year history. Critics pointed out that, since the crisis was a crisis of the private sector, not of the government, cutting government spending and raising interest rates was simply reducing demand in the economy and driving even sound firms into bankruptcy. Under such criticism, even the notoriously impervious Fund has revised its approach, easing its policies considerably in all of the Asian crash countries and encouraging a high level of deficit spending to reflate the economy. However, enormous damage had already been done, and is clearly visible in the shape of needlessly bankrupt firms and millions of extra unemployed.

Jeffrey Sachs graphically claims that, 'Instead of dousing the flames, the IMF in effect screamed fire in the theatre.' By opting to demand widespread structural reforms and in effect declaring large parts of the (Asian) economy rotten, the Fund precipitated a crisis by demanding huge reforms.

Fund-style stabilisation and long-term adjustment work to a completely different rhythm. Stabilisation, especially when the problem is one of liquidity, requires a rapid restoration of confidence with a low-conditionality bridging loan and a debt rescheduling. It means acting fast and providing large sums of money up front. Structural adjustment, on the other hand, is a longer-term reworking of the regulation of the economy which requires a sense of local ownership, a prolonged period of debate, dialogue and technical assistance. Such reforms are best carried out when the economy is in a good state, since some people inevitably lose out and public support for reform can easily be eroded by a recession.

Since the threat of suspending loan disbursements is the Fund's preferred means of exerting leverage on governments, loans are handed over in small amounts over prolonged periods of time, with doubt surrounding whether the country will qualify for the next tranche, i.e. the exact opposite of what is required to restore confidence. This was a weakness accepted in the IMF's internal evaluation of its handling of the Asia crisis. The Contingency Credit Line was established at the Fund's April 1999 meeting to try and get around this problem by introducing pre-qualification for crisis-loans – countries would qualify in advance of any crisis by introducing the necessary reforms during times of economic plenty.

While foreign investors and local elites enjoyed most of the gains of the pre-crisis period, they have had to bear very little of the costs of the crash. Instead, these have fallen on the poor and middle-income groups. Besides the simple, but important point that this asymmetric distribution of pain and gain is unjust, there are some important moral hazard implications. In financial parlance, moral hazard means that lenders and borrowers are not made to bear the cost of poor investment decisions, thereby making it more likely that they will make similar mistakes in the future, thereby generating further crises. At an international level, foreign investors have found that they will be bailed out by the international financial institutions (i.e. Western taxpayers) when the going gets rough. At a national level, elites have seen that debts can be socialised – passed on in turn to their own taxpayers and workers. The issue of how to 'bail in' investors to debt work-out packages is extremely complex, and, according to British civil servants, has provoked more arguments within the IMF Board of Directors than any other issue. *The Economist* believes the Clinton administration has simply given up on it, in the face of opposition from Wall Street.

In the previous chapter we explained the inordinate influence of the US on the IMF. However, the Asia crisis may mark a new low in the Fund's reputation as a vehicle for US aspirations – the Korean rescue package included a raft of conditions (such as opening up the economy to imported auto parts) which had precious little to do with the country's balance of payments problems, but had been persistent US demands in bilateral trade negotiations for much of the 1990s. One negotiator reportedly said that the US had achieved more in six months of crisis bailout talks than in ten years of bilateral trade negotiations.

Following the Brazilian currency crisis of January 1999, the World Bank's safety net programme also ran into controversy when the Brazilian government claimed it had secured loans worth some $3.45 billion from the World Bank and Inter-American Development Bank (IDB) which would be spent on reforms and social programmes. The Bank claimed that its loan would 'support the government's efforts to protect social expenditure to the poor.' Instead, Brazilian NGOs and legislators found that the money was in fact to be spent on debt service payments. The social connection was merely that the loan's disbursement was made conditional on the Brazilian government protecting, as far as possible, spending on 22 social programmes which were judged to be of particular importance. Even this guarantee was not what it seemed, since spending on many of the programmes already enjoyed automatic protection under the Brazilian constitution. So the Bank provided no new money for social spending; the programmes were in any case cut by some 6% (although the Bank claimed in a letter that they would have been cut more in the absence of its loan) and yet both the Bank and the Brazilian government claimed to be arranging extra loans for social protection.

While all IFI's pay lip service to poverty alleviation, the financial crises of the last two decades demonstrate that social issues remain an afterthought in the minds of policy makers.

A new challenge confronts the struggle to end world poverty: the growing size and instability of international financial markets. Since the Mexican *peso* crash of 1994, a series of financial crises have threatened the hopes and livelihoods of millions of the world's poor. There is substantial evidence that rapid financial deregulation leads not to growth but to greater economic volatility and social inequality. Financial systems should be at the service of the real economy, and the economy at the service of the population, not the other way around. Changes in the international financial architecture should seek to reorient financial flows to the South in the interest of long-term sustainable development. The IMF and World Bank should restrain from policies outlined above which legitimately are the purview of sovereign countries, based on broad national social consensus. Current official proposals for reform of the international financial architecture are based on the erroneous assumption that capital account liberalisation and financial deregulation are both inevitable and desirable. Instead of pressing for more liberalisation, IFIs should be assessing the merits of different approaches to RE-regulate global finance to bring it back under some form of democratic control.

## Hot money

(Edited from Dillon, 1998)

The 1998 Business Forum of the Americas advocated 'effective measures for free transfer' of financial assets across national borders. This could mean more freedom for corporations to repatriate profits and capital investments beyond the regulation of capital flows already established under NAFTA.

Before cross-border capital flows are further liberalised, the history of the 1994-95 Mexico *peso* crisis, the 1997 Asian financial crisis and the 1998-99 Brazilian and Russian crises should be taken into account. These crises demonstrated the destabilising effect of excessive inflows and outflows of short-term capital investment. NAFTA contributed to the Mexican crisis by making it difficult for Mexico to put controls on hot money.

Over a five year period, from 1989 to 1994, almost ¾ of the US$98 billion worth of foreign investment that entered Mexico was short-term portfolio investment, that is, purchases of bonds... Only 27% of the money that flowed into Mexico was direct investment. Even so, this direct investment did not create many new jobs since much of it was for the purchase of privatised state enterprises.

During the 1994-95 crisis investors took over US$48.6 billion worth of portfolio investment out of Mexico. The Mexican government was forced to turn to the IMF and the US and Canadian governments for an emergency bailout package worth about US$48 billion. Citizens (taxpayers) of the US and Canada were not consulted.

The primary beneficiaries of this bailout were the currency speculators and lenders of hot money who were reimbursed by the Mexican government. The Mexican people were saddled with an immense debt and harsh austerity policies. Mexico's external debt rose from US$132 billion at the end of 1993 to US$166 billion in 1995 (World Bank).

Chile was one Latin American country that escaped the 'tequila effect' that destabilised Latin financial markets in the wake of the Mexican crisis. One reason Chile's finances remained stable is because its *encaje* system required foreign investors to deposit a portion of the capital they brought into the country in an interest free account with the central bank. Furthermore, foreign portfolio investment had to remain within the country for one year. While Chile temporarily suspended the *encaje* [...] its experience demonstrates the efficacy of such controls in mitigating financial turmoil.

In the wake of the Asian financial crisis a debate has opened up on how best to cool down hot money. Finance Ministers are debating how to prevent private investors from precipitously withdrawing their investments and precipitating or exacerbating financial crises. Instead of bailing out private investors with public funds as occurred in Mexico, Asia and most recently Brazil, ministers are discussing how to make private investors bear part (why not all?) of the costs of resolving the financial crises.

Trade ministers' discussions of further liberalisation of cross-border financial flows may contradict the efforts of financial ministers to find ways to cool down hot money. Private financial firms view trade pacts like the FTAA as opportunities to head off efforts to re-establish some kind of capital controls. However, the historical evidence shows that excessive international financial flows do not lead to an efficient use of funds but rather to manias, crises and panic.

## Capital flight

One of the problems associated with international investment has been that funds flowing into a country for alleged development purposes often flows right back out as capital flight. Instead of putting international loans to use in building the nation's infrastructure, manufacturing base or spurring demand for domestic goods and services, in many instances the funds end up in foreign bank accounts, property, investments or US Treasury bonds. Former Citicorp chairperson, Walter Wriston has observed that 'most people believe that the flight of capital from Latin America on deposit in New York and Miami exceeds total capital remaining in those countries.'

Perhaps the most infamous stories of capital flight involve leaders of poor nations who managed to create personal fortunes that rank among the world's largest. Latin America's past military dictators' bribes received from foreign contractors and kickbacks on government contracts – funded largely with foreign loans – figure predominantly in the amassed wealth of these leaders. The then Zairean kleptocracy of Mobutu Seko and deposed Philippines dictator Ferdinand Marcos stand out worldwide. More recently, the current Peruvian President, Alberto Fujimori, is rumored to have absconded abroad (in failed Asian investments) some US$9 billion garnered from sales of state enterprises to foreign investors.

Capital flight reduces foreign exchange reserves for the debtor countries, thus exacerbating external debt problems. It undermines economic stability and growth by aggravating fiscal deficits and by reducing tax revenues and domestic investment. Sizeable capital outflows associated with drug money laundering must also be included.

Capital flight often worsens the distribution of wealth within developing countries. Southern private citizens who invest capital overseas may benefit from doing so, but these profits are not typically repatriated or distributed evenly within their home countries. Furthermore, since capital flight reduces the tax base of developing countries, the poor pay a greater portion of the burden of taxation and economic adjustment. Southern nations' political and economic elites who hold personal assets abroad have a stake in the current international financial system, which may help to explain why so few debtor nations have failed to declare a debt default or payment moratorium.

Capital flight in the 1990s remains a problem in relation to capital inflows because international banks have reduced new lending and direct foreign investments are down world wide, especially following the Asian crisis. One interesting but probably unrealistic 'solution' proposed by advocates of debt relief would allow Northern banks to seize the assets of Southern elites in their vaults in a corresponding write-off of sovereign debts.

# Chapter 5
# The more we pay the more we owe

Through the 1989 US Brady Plan, commercial banks reduced up to 35% of the debt owed to them by middle-income countries. The banks were further supported by the IFIs and individual creditor countries with official guarantees on the remaining outstanding loans. Thus, the Brady Plan shifted risk from commercial creditors to public ones at the cost of the Northern taxpayers and Southern populations' well-being.

Bilateral donors, especially the Paris Club creditors, were the first to provide debt relief in the early 1980s and since the G-7/8 Cologne meeting in mid-1999 significantly more debt relief has been promised, but again tied to structural adjustment conditions – the US has promised over US$123 million debt relief, with the UK pledging around US$221 million and the EU some 1 billion euros. While Japan is also a creditor nation, in late 1999 it took on a new US$167 billion debt itself, raising its ratio of debt to GDP to 122.5%, the highest among the creditor Northern countries. It hopes this will help it and other Asian neighbours recover from the crisis in 1997-98.

Until HIPC I in 1996, the IFIs did not allow rescheduling or cancellation of their loans – although in practice they did so in some cases by refinancing hard loans (at market interest rates) with soft loans (at below market rates). This initiative also requires structural adjustment programmes and tellingly, since 1997 the World Bank's annual debt tables have been renamed Global Development Finance.

In summary, the 1990s saw very little growth in debt owed to Paris Club members and commercial banks and a high level of debt growth to IFIs. Latin America and the Caribbean's situation at the end of the decade was one where old debts had been re-programmed and new debts were mostly directed toward the private sector or via IFIs to the public sector. The region is wallowing in sovereign multilateral debt.

The Asian crisis affected the whole world, including the Latin American/Caribbean region – all countries redoubled their efforts on export growth policies. The late century impact of the Asian crisis on regional exports and debt service capacity demonstrates the vulnerabilities in the current dominant economic paradigm. As a whole, the region grew about 3% during the last decade, far less than before the 1980s debt and late 1990s Asian capital flows crises.

Table 2 Total debt, total payments

| | 1980 | 1990 | 2000 |
|---|---|---|---|
| Total LA/C debt | US$191 billion | US$480 billion | US$750 billion |
| Total debt service paid | US$350 billion ('80-90) | | US$815 billion ('90-99) |

In short, the region paid US$1.165 *trillion* in debt service over the last two decades of the century and still owed Northern creditors US$750 billion at the end of the millennium (García, 1999).

Southern debt (Africa, Asia and Latin America/Caribbean) overall in 1980 was US$610 billion. In 1997 it reached US$2.3 trillion.

Three outstanding debt/finance crises stand out in the 1990s in the Latin American region. The early 1999 Brazil monetary crisis, tied to the Asian financial crisis, has been repeatedly referred to throughout this text and is still evolving. The mid-decade Mexican banking crisis and late 1999 Ecuador Brady Bonds 'bailouts' require more attention.

Mexico's peso crisis in 1994 has led to an ongoing banking crisis since 1995. 'This has been an awful time, because we've had to cope with the worst crisis of the past 50 years and the opening of the Mexican market to foreign capital at the same time,' lamented the director general of the Banco Nacional de Mexico. 'But the problem is a lot bigger than the banks. A failed recovery could cripple an economy just reviving from the devastating peso crisis that precipitated a $50 billion international bailout. Already, Mexico's recovery is showing strains, as the country grapples with rising private sector debt and a fast growing current account' (Willoughby and Conger, 1998).

The government bailout of the seriously weakened Mexican banking system has been coupled with mergers and foreign assumption of many of the country's top banks. During the debt crisis of the 1980s, 'then Mexican president Portillo had nationalized all but two of the country's 60 banks [...] Bankers lost the discipline of making and collecting loans. Virtually all credit was allocated by the (Mexican) Treasury and most loans were made to state-owned companies [...] Essentially, bankers gathered deposits for the government and those deposits benefited from an exceedingly generous insurance program – with all corporate and consumer deposits unconditionally guaranteed, without limitation (moral hazard)' (Ibid).

The Salinas government came to power in 1988 set on liberalising the economy, selling off state enterprises and re-privatising the financial sector by auctioning off regional and national banks. By 1995, Mexico was in its

67

## Table 3 Debt service paid as % of GDP and exports

Latinamerica Press Special Debt Issue with
statistics compiled by Jubilee 2000

|  | % GDP | % Exports |
|---|---|---|
| Argentina | 6 | 59 |
| Bolivia | 6 | 35 |
| Brazil | 5 | 57 |
| Chile | 6 | 20 |
| Colombia | 5 | 27 |
| Ecuador | 10 | 31 |
| El Salvador | 3 | 7 |
| Guatemala | 2 | 10 |
| Guyana | 17 | 18 |
| Haiti | 1 | 16 |
| Honduras | 11 | 21 |
| Jamaica | 17 | 16 |
| Mexico | 13 | 32 |
| Nicaragua | 17 | 36 |
| Panama | 20 | 17 |
| Peru | 5 | 31 |
| Venezuela | 13 | 31 |

Note: Economists claim that less than 20% of export earnings should be applied to debt service payments, but eleven of the region's most important economies surpass that, while four more hover very near – the export led growth model of 'development' seems designed to specifically 'allow' debtors to service their debts at their own economic jeopardy.

worst recession in 60 years. Despite 7% growth in 1997, the real wage of Mexicans was below 1994 levels in 2000.

During the banking crisis, Northern investors and banks such as Goldman, Sachs & Co. and Bankers Trust paid 50 cents on the dollar for loans with a combined face value of US$17 million, so-called debt swaps. Later loan auctions yielded prices as low as 17 cents on the dollar. Selling the loans at a loss meant the government (Mexican and Northern taxpayers through the IMF and bilateral deals) had to pick up the tab for what the banks didn't write off or swap.

In late 1998, the Mexican Congress did pass a new Law for the Protection of Bank Savings, which provided for the curtailment of the government's previous near-blanket guarantee of bank liabilities but also eliminated all restrictions on foreign ownership of the largest Mexican banks. The IMF also required that at least 1% of Mexican GDP be allocated to pay the real portion of the cost of the accumulated debt bail-out. And there is a new government agency responsible for liability coverage and which will need annual congressional approval for its budget, which was not previously the case. But despite these perceived improvements in the system, the Mexican financial sector's return to good health was hindered by the Asian and Brazilian crises. And the total bailout adds up to an estimated at US$100 billion.

'It is difficult to determine what the country's costs would have been if the government had allowed the whole banking system to fail, or if it had re-nationalised the system for the second time in 15 years [...] Of the 18 intervened banks, four have been sold to a third party; four are still pending to be cleaned up and then sold; and the remaining institutions are undergoing liquidation' (*Standard and Poor's Credit Week*). The newly-created Institute for the Protection of Bank Savings (IPAB) was handling these transactions. IPAB had to decide the future of pending bank mergers and auctions, which determines the future of Mexico's banking system. But lending is shrinking. 'Banking in Mexico remains a tough business. Patience has become a virtue in the current banking environment [...] Banking is a long-term business. And Mexico – with the free trade agreement – must get successfully closer to North America' (Conger, 1999). Meanwhile the purchasing power of the average Mexican citizen has dropped 24% since NAFTA began operating in 1994. In late 1999 the World Bank announced a new US$1.1 billion loan for banking decentralisation.

## Table 4 Overview of debt in Latin America and the Caribbean

|  | Total Debt US $ billion | Debt Service Paid | Per Capita Debt |
|---|---|---|---|
| Argentina | 147 (1) | 17.5 billion | 4,026 |
| Bolivia | 5.2 | 475 million | 656 |
| Brazil | 257 (2) | 75.7 billion (3) | 1,300 |
| Chile | 31.4 | 4.4 billion | 2,096 |
| Colombia | 31.8 | 4.5 billion | 836 |
| Cuba (4) |  |  |  |
| Ecuador | 17 | 1.8 billion | 1,243 |
| El Salvador | 3.3 | 279 million | 547 |
| Guatemala | 4.1 | 362 million | 371 |
| Guyana | 1.4 | 133 million | 1,609 |
| Haiti | 1.1 | 35 million | 151 |
| Honduras | 4.7 | 505 million (5) | 783 |
| Jamaica | 4.1 | 641 million (6) | 1,304 |
| Mexico | 149.7 | 32.5 billion | 1,576 |
| Nicaragua | 5.7 | 326 million | 1,135 |
| Panama | 7.7 | 670 million | 2,572 |
| Peru | 30.5 | 2.25 billion | 1,220 |
| Venezuela | 35.5 | 4.6 billion | 1,545 (7) |

(1) Argentina has 350% more foreign debt in 1999 than in 1989.

(2) Public debt rose 48% in 1999 due to the devaluation of the Brazilian currency, the *real*.

(3) Some interest rates at the end of 1999 were as high as 25.5%.

(4) Cuban non-Russian foreign debt is now US$11.2 billion, over half of which is owed to Japan, Spain and France; there are no Paris Club loans since the US has veto power there.

(5) Debt service is double what Honduras invests in its health and education sectors combined.

(6) Jamaica has the highest ratio of debt service to GNP in the region at 17.1%. Combined health and education budgets comes only to 10.7%.

(7) As we can see, absolute debt figures tell us very little in terms of human impact – as seen in the per capita figures in Bolivia, Haiti, Guyana, Jamaica, Honduras and Nicaragua, relatively low debt in absolute figures but devastating economically.

## The Failure of the Mexico Bailout

(Exerpted from the Development Gap)

Since financial crisis hit Asia in late 1997 and the IMF intervened in Thailand, Indonesia and then South Korea, the 1995 bailout of Mexico and of those investors holding short-term Mexican bonds has been held up by US and Mexican policymakers as a successful model to be replicated. Indeed, a picture has been painted of a rapidly recovering Mexican economy that is regaining the status of a fundamentally healthy emerging market which it held in many quarters until the *peso* and the economy collapsed at the end of 1994.

The reality is quite different. From the perspective of most Mexicans, who continue to suffer under the intensified adjustment programme on which the bailout was conditioned, and of Mexican economists and citizens' organisations that relate to the real economy, their country remains in serious economic straits. The best that can be said is that the level of suffering and economic insecurity of the majority of the population has stabilised for the moment. At the same time, however, the core of Mexico's economy has been gutted, the same conditions which created the 1994 crash are reappearing, and the country has been destabilised from the bottom up, as much in Mexico City as in the mountains of Chiapas.

• Domestic productive capacity has collapsed. Between 1995 and 1997, more than a third of Mexico's businesses – over 20,000 small and medium-sized enterprises – declared bankruptcy. With domestic demand still low, interest rates still high and barriers to imports falling, there has so far been no recovery in this core sector of the Mexican economy.

71

• Massive unemployment persists. Two million people lost their jobs in the economic collapse, leaving one third of the economically active population of nearly 30 million workers unemployed or in precarious jobs. Some 1.8 million peasants have been forced to leave their land in search of work. The absence of unemployment benefits has exacerbated this crisis. The government recently announced the creation of a million new jobs in 1997, but with anyone working one day per month classified officially as employed, it is difficult to determine the significance of this figure.

• Wages have fallen precipitously. Over the past three years, real wages, already perilously low, have declined by almost 25 percent. Since 1982, wages have lost more than 66 percent of their purchasing power.

• The banking system remains virtually insolvent. Only periodic injections of fresh capital from the Mexican government keep the banks afloat. Since the collapse of the economy, the government has invested the equivalent of more than US$46 billion in the banking system, an amount equivalent to 12% of the country's GDP and twice the amount spent by the government on education and social development combined. More than 50% of the banks' portfolios are overdue, as most businesses and consumers cannot repay their loans.

• The current account is once again in deficit. The trade deficits in December and January were worse than expected. Virtually the only sector which has shown any growth since 1994 is export manufacturing, particularly the *maquilas*. As this sector is now highly dependent on the import of capital goods and components for assembly, the structural problem that was brought on by economic liberalisation and that contributed to the 1994 crisis is reappearing.

• Interest payments on heavy foreign borrowing have exacerbated the current account deficit. In order to pay back the US Treasury bailout loan, the Mexican government borrowed extensively in international private markets. It offered rates of five percent above what is normal, taking on extensive obligations. Today, a large percentage of Mexico's reserves are borrowed monies, an extremely precarious situation, even by IMF standards.

• Mexico will have to begin relying again on speculative capital to reduce the deficit. The current account imbalance increased steadily through 1998 and nearly doubled the size of 1997's deficit. By 2000 it should be approaching 1994 levels. Direct investment would be insufficient to fill this gap even without the current insecurities being felt by emerging-market investors. Furthermore, agreements signed by the Mexican government in the context of NAFTA mean that no controls can be placed on capital flows, making the Mexican economy ever more vulnerable.

• Increased poverty and inequality have destabilised Mexican society. The OECD has warned that Mexico's economic crisis and the adjustment measures prescribed by the IMF to address it had increased social inequality. Intense and pervasive poverty, extreme economic inequities, and a growing desperation and alienation have engendered an increasingly violent response on the part of Mexicans to their current circumstances. Crime in Mexico City and other urban centres has proliferated under the 'bailout economy', making it one of the country's major preoccupations. The drug trade continues at ever expanding levels.

First in Chiapas and then in other southern states, rebel movements have taken up arms to challenge the government and policies that have kept local populations in poverty.

The economic policies imposed upon South Korea, Indonesia and Thailand are similar to the structural adjustment policies which brought the Mexican economy to the point of ruin in 1994 and that have continued to be imposed with increased intensity. Policies of austerity, wage suppression and high interest rates and the rapid opening of the economy even before Mexican enterprises and institutions had developed the capacity to compete in the global economy and to manage increased financial flows effectively have been promoted and warmly welcomed by foreign investors. These measures do not, however, enable Mexico to build the basis of a strong domestic economy and to escape the destructive cycle in which it now finds itself. This is hardly a model for Asians or anyone else to follow.

*This analysis was prepared by The Development GAP in consultation with Mexican economists Alejandro Nadal (Colegio de México), Rocio Mejía (Advisor, Mexican Senate) and Carlos Heredia (Member of Congress – Cámara de Diputados) and with input provided by Mexican citizens' organizations and networks, including Equipo PUEBLO, Red Mexicana de Acción frente al Libre Comercio, and El Barzón.*

## Ecuador

(Edited from LatinAmerica Press Special Issue on the Debt Crisis,1999)

An event which caught the attention of the international financial community was Ecuador's announcement in September 1999 that it would not complete in full the upcoming payments due on its Brady Bonds, which account for about half the country's foreign debt. Earlier in the year, the government perpetrated the folly of using 40% of its monetary reserves to bailout one of the country's largest banks. This set off gross speculation in the national currency which within less that two months lost more than 100% of its value, setting off an inflation rate of 65% (the highest in the region) and raising interest rates to 90% annually. This banking crisis cost the government some US$1.7 billion, and the country was facing paying debt service and Brady Bond interests later in the year. In the first nine months of 1999, the

Ecuadoran banking and financial system lost US$348.5 million and over 200,000 jobs.

Indeed, in September, Ecuador announced it would suspend interest payment on at least half of its US$6 billion-worth of Brady Bonds. This was the first time 'Bradies' were put 'on hold' by any country. However, 'there should be no contagion [...] Ecuador is a special case that can be differentiated from other Latin nations because its economic and financial fundamentals are poor, the country is over-indebted [...] On the basis of links for contagion...Ecuador is too small...' The drama was played out in the midst of a heated debate about how costs could be shared between bondholders and IFIs. 'Ecuadorans defaulted because they were egged on by Washington as part of burden sharing' (Conger 1999b). 'The perceived rationale for a default would be to answer critics of the IMF , especially creditor countries, who allege that the Fund abets moral hazard by consistently stepping in to prevent sovereign defaults, offering a kind of indirect guarantee to private investors. Private investors shun the idea of a default, which would bail them in to restructuring debt, which is properly called 'burden sharing. The IMF is ... choosing countries with an external debt amount small enough not to cause panic in international financial markets' (Conger 1999a).

Even if the IMF is finally recognising the perils of moral hazard, Ecuador must still formulate a structural adjustment program, starting with spending cuts, in order to get IMF support. At the end of December the IMF indeed approved a US$1.2 billion loan, a mere third of which was earmarked for alleged social programs.

Of US$98 million dollars due in Brady Bonds in September, Ecuador paid US$48 million, or less than half. 'We will only pay those Brady Bond interests that are not guaranteed,' declared the government. The US Treasury guaranteed much of the Brady Bonds and Ecuador's president continued, 'The money is there but we (the government) can't use it. But, the creditors (bond holders) can operationalise that guarantee' (Los Tiempos, 9/27/99). A month later Ecuador also announced a moratorium on payments on Eurobonds, worth some US$27 million in interest. Ecuador had decided to renegotiate all its debt. Meanwhile, so-called vultures are buying up Ecuador's bonds at about 22 cents on the dollar.

## 'Don't lend us *ANY MORE*'

### Life after a moratorium on debt payments

(Edited from Saavedra, 1999)

'Here is a serious country, acting in good faith, that wants to fulfil its international commitments, but has difficulty making payments – not because it doesn't want to pay, but because it cannot pay,' President Jamil Mahuad said in August 1999, when he announced that Ecuador would not pay interest due on Brady bonds, part of the external debt that represented 42% of the country's 1999 budget and is expected to account for 54 % in 2000. Following the same policy, in October the government decided not to pay interest due on Eurobonds, constituting a virtual moratorium on service of its external debt of about US$16.5 billion, in an attempt to force a re-negotiation that would allow it to reduce the total amount and exchange current debt papers for 20-year 'global' bonds.

The government's decision received substantial support within the country. The decision also received the tacit approval of the IMF. Ecuador's debt is distributed among Brady bonds, Eurobonds and multilateral creditors. The Brady bonds have the greatest face value but the lowest current value – 30 cents on the dollar – in the financial market. In the end, optimism was deflated by reality. Mahuad's announcement caused a drop in bond prices, and 'vultures' – speculators who purchase devalued debt with the intention of suing the issuing country for the full face value – took advantage. Such speculators have acquired 25 percent of Ecuador's debt papers at about 22 cents per dollar.

The present crisis occurred because Ecuador's creditors in the 1990s were not the same ones who were involved in the 1980s, when the Brady Plan allowed for an exchange of bonds at a discount from the debt's face value. Then, the creditors were commercial banks or financial institutions which could be pressured to negotiate by the governments of their countries, which could also force them to take significant losses in the process. Now, however, the creditors are firms or individuals who have purchased government bonds in the private capital market, with no clauses obligating private creditors to accept proposals for debt restructuring.

Various mechanisms for addressing the debt problem have been suggested, ranging from repurchasing debt papers in the secondary market to giving Brady bondholders a stake in state-owned companies, turning the debt papers into stock shares. But an economic analyst and advisor to the Co-ordinating Committee of Social Movements sees the need for a more comprehensive solution. 'This is the best moment to renegotiate the external debt and seek a definite agreement on the basis of national interests, and not just a patch readjusted to the creditors' desires,' Acosta said.

A radical possibility, Acosta added, would be to stop borrowing. 'There's no reason to be alarmed about a possible cut-off of credit to Ecuador, because most has already been cut. Therefore, we can propose that they let us grow and say that we will pay the debt, but after a 50-year grace period during which we can restructure our economy and create conditions that will allow us to pay the debt without the present social cost. 'Meanwhile,' he added, 'please don't lend us any more.'

## Jamaica: when debt begins at home

Unlike most Latin American and Caribbean nations, more than half of Jamaica's staggering debt is owed to internal creditors.

The Caribbean 'paradise' of Jamaica appears a laid-back, tranquil place where people happily go about their lives under sunny skies, surrounded by blue waters. Appearances, however, can be deceptive. In late April 1999, the island nation erupted in a four-day frenzy of violence which left nine people dead and scores injured, and caused millions of dollars in damage. The catalyst was an announced hike in fuel prices, but observers blame an economy shattered by debt.

Debt is an important issue in Jamaica, but unlike most developing countries, the island suffers more from the weight of internal than external debt. Of Jamaica's US$7 billion debt, 56% is owed to lenders inside the country. This has not always been the case. In 1993, when the country's debt was valued at about $3 billion, the domestic component was just over 10%. But a poor credit rating forced Jamaica's government to borrow from domestic creditors, worsening the situation because of high domestic interest rates, which hover around 13%, but in the past have been as high as 40%.

For average Jamaicans, however, debt is debt, whether the money is owed to creditors inside the country or abroad, because the effects are the same. In 1999, Prime Minister Patterson's government allocated a whopping 87% of total expenditure for debt-service payments, leaving just 13% for health, social services, education and other needs. The government has professed its commitment to sustaining social spending, but to do that it must again approach lenders, preferably those in foreign markets.

Many observers say the average Jamaican still fails to appreciate the seriousness of the impact of the debt on his or her everyday life — a fact some blame on the ineffectiveness of the country's campaign against the debt. Jamaica's Jubilee campaign against the debt, which began in 1998, was

slow to react and only in the late 1990s began to take into accou
staggering consequences of internal debt. Activists believe that Jamai
precarious condition qualifies it for debt forgiveness, conversion and other
measures under HIPC. Alleviating the roughly $3.5 billion foreign debt
would help the island nation convert its high-interest internal loans to more
manageable external debt.

## Peru

(Excerpt from Boyd, 1999)

Accuracy of statistics is of paramount importance in the debt-reduction
debate.

'How much would it cost to reduce poverty in Peru to zero? To eliminate
Peru's extreme poverty would cost US$332 million a year. How much do we
pay (to reduce) the debt? Five times that amount,' says Peruvian economist
Javier Iguíñiz.

What frustrates Peru's anti-debt campaigners is that although the country's
total external debt is more than $1,200 per person, or $30 billion in total —
$10 billion more than in the 1980s and growing, with 20 to 25% of the
national budget going to debt service — the country is not considered part
of the World Bank and G-7 nations' scheme for debt reduction (HIPC). For
debt activists from countries excluded from the initiative, like Peru, HIPC
has been a disappointment. Peru is considered a medium-income country.
Critics say the government has inflated the figure to make the country more
attractive to foreign investors. Iguíñiz says calculations should consider social
indicators, like the amount spent on debt service compared to spending on
health, education and social security. Using the most recent statistics and
indicators, such as the number of people living on a dollar a day, infant
mortality and spending on public services, Iguíñiz says, puts Peru on par
with the region's poorest countries: Haiti, Honduras and Bolivia. If the poverty
line, adjusted for the cost of living, is considered an income of $2 a day, he
adds, 49% of Peru's population, about 12 million people, live below the
poverty level, a higher percentage than in Honduras, at 47%, or Nicaragua,
at 44% — both HIPC countries.

# The debt is unpayable

... South's debts were contracted by illegitimate governments.

... 980s much of ... African debt was contracted by dictatorships, with the full knowledge of the creditor lenders. Most of these funds were not invested in the public's interest, even though average people are expected to bear the brunt of repayment.

The creditors' repayment requirements are unethical.

Unemployment, reduced spending on health and education and other social services are the direct results of debt servicing. No law or contract should be legally binding when to comply results in disproportionate harm.
Northern creditors and their institutions have already been fairly compensated.

(From Iriarte, 1999)

Repayment interest rates are above the market norm which are unethical and often usurious and due to their variable levels, often doubled or tripled the original debt incurred. In the same period the debtors' terms of trade have declined and the dollar became overvalued, which means Latin America has had a net negative transfer of funds from South to North of approximately US$40 billion annually for more than 25 years.

To pay the debt in full means grave economic dislocation and increased poverty for the Southern debtors.

Ever worse terms of trade for the South mean ever greater economic advantage for the North. Much of the original debt returned North due to capital flight and interest rates were higher than the norm. Taking these factors into account, not only has the debt been repaid, but one can calculate that the North owes the South.

# Chapter 6
## ...the less we have

In the 1990s, increasing poverty in Latin America was built on centuries old colonial social structures, and was reinforced by neo-liberal economic policies. Perhaps the greatest and most nefarious myth of globalisation is that it will, or even can, improve human wellbeing for any but a minuscule minority of the world's population. More than 80% of the world suffers from these forces but do not participate in their benefits. One analyst has calculated that only those economies with per capita incomes of more than US$10,000 can even hope to come out ahead.

There are scores of other books which deal specifically with poverty and/ or development and the reader interested in those issues separately should pursue them. This chapter is more focused on how the debt and other global financial crises, and the fundamentally flawed and dominant export-led growth model of development, have increased poverty and inequality. What began as a debt and banking crisis in the 1980s, later created other types of exigencies. The accumulated social costs generated by SAPs have been enormous and devastating, particularly for the poor, since the distribution of the burden of adjustment has been skewed against them. Government cuts, particularly in education, health, housing and other social services, have affected the poor disproportionately, given their greater reliance on such services and their inability to afford the substitutes provided by the private sector.

During the first half of the 1990s, there were some successes in reducing poverty but setbacks were registered after the 1994 Mexican peso crisis and later after the 1997-98 Asian crisis. In addition, the greater reliance on the market has intensified traditional inequality in Latin American income distribution. There has been an increase in both absolute and relative poverty, now greater than during the 1980s so-called 'lost development decade,' according to CEPAL, the UN's Economic Commission for Latin America and the Caribbean. The general deterioration of living standards for the vast majority has generated social tensions as evidenced by the increase of civil crime and violence. The more dramatic IMF riots of the 1980s were replaced in the 1990s by a deeply felt social malaise. One African debt expert coined the alternative reading of the IMF acronym as the Institute for Misery and Famine.

Globalisation has left entire countries, regions, ethnic groups , economic classes and most often women as victims of greater inequality. More than 70 countries are poorer at the end of the century than 20 years earlier. The reign of the free market has brought poverty for the majority, especially in the South. Globalisation is more than burgeoning capital flows and trade in goods and services. It is also the ever increasing interdependence not only of economic factors but also cultural, technological and government structures. The collapse of the Thai currency not only affected Southeast Asia but also negatively influenced the economies of Latin America and Africa. Globalisation is not new to history but this time around it does represent certain special attributes: stock market and capital flows of unprecedented scale and speed; new modes of communication such as the Internet; new organisations such as the WTO, TNCs, international NGOs and other groups which transcend national borders and interests; and more multilateral agreements which subvert national sovereignty.

The opening of national borders to greater capital flows, trade, and information has not brought greater respect for international human rights, including human development and poverty alleviation. Competitive markets do not promote equality or well-being for the majority of the world's population. Rather, they concentrate power and wealth among a small minority of people, countries and companies, leaving the rest at the margins. When the market loses control, as in the Asian crisis, the consequences are global. Unbridled profit motives raise ethical concerns by sacrificing justice and equality.

Ironically, but tellingly, greater involvement in globalisation means greater poverty. Latin America and Africa export something like 30% of their GNP while the OECD countries export about 10% less. But the terms of trade for the South are their lowest in 150 years. More than 80 Southern countries today have lower per capita incomes than a decade ago. Moreover, more and more people are unemployed as globalisation requires new skills not easily available in the South. Inequality among countries is also increasing. The income difference between the 20% of the world's population that lives in the richest countries and the poorest 20% in the South was 30 to 1 in 1960, 60 to 1 in 1990 and 70 to 1 in 1997, a startling but revealing trend. At the end of the century the world's richest 20% of the population enjoyed 86% of global GDP while the poorest 20% struggled with a mere 1%. The 200 richest people in the world doubled their incomes from 1994-98. The three richest *individuals* in the world have combined wealth greater than the 48 least developed countries and their 600 million inhabitants. The wave of acquisitions and mergers is concentrating industrial power at the risk of eliminating competition. In 1998, the world's 10 largest telecommunications companies controlled 86% of that global market worth US$262 billion.

'If there is a single defining feature of globalisation in the late 20th century, it is the increasing ease with which technology can and does accompany capital flows across borders. The nature of connectivity threatens to irrevocably sever the link between high productivity, high technology and high wages. It is now possible for TNCs to combine through their investment activity high productivity, high technology and low wages' (Watkins, 1997). More than 13 million people lost their jobs as a result of the Asian crisis and those who were lucky enough to still have employment found their wages reduced some 40-60%. During the 1990s, employment in the informal sector rose globally to 58%, with 85% of all new jobs in this category, with no fixed incomes, no social benefits and no stability. In 1996 alone, the percentage of workers with no job contracts or other guarantees rose 30% in Chile, 36% in Argentina, 39% in Colombia and 41% in Peru.

Table 5 Income distribution in some Latin American countries (UNDP, 1999) % GDP

|  | Poorest 20% | Richest 20% |
| --- | --- | --- |
| Uruguay | 5 | 48.7 |
| Costa Rica | 4.3 | 50.6 |
| Peru | 4.4 | 51.3 |
| Ecuador | 2.3 | 59.6 |
| Brazil | 2.5 | 63.4 |
| Paraguay | 2.3 | 62.3 |

# The chance to work

More than 150 million people (33% of the population) in Latin America survive on less than US$2/day.

According to the IDB, Latin America has the most inequitable income distribution in the world and it is now worse than 20 years ago – if Latin America had an income distribution equivalent to Southeast Asia, there would be 20% less poverty in the region. One quarter of Latin American wealth is in the hands of 5% of the population; the poorest 30% of the population receives 7.5% of income. Brazil, Chile, Guatemala, Ecuador, Mexico, Panama and Paraguay have the most skewed income distributions

According to the ILO (International Labour Organisation) 1999 Latin America Report:

- child labour affects up to 19% of children aged 10 to 14 in Latin America
- unemployment overall is higher than during the 1980s debt crisis
- wages have lost 27% of their real value between 1980 and 1998
- 85% of new 'jobs' in the region are in the informal sector
- Female unemployment is 60% higher than for males
- Between 1990-98 employment grew by 2.9% but the labour force grew by 3.1%

- Brazilian unemployment represents 5% of the world's total – in 1986 it ranked 13th in world wide unemployment; in 1999 it was 4th highest, surpassed only by India, Indonesia and Russia.

## Haiti rebound

(Excerpted from Miles and Ries, 2000)

The informal economy in Haiti has become a survival system in a country with a 70% unemployment rate and 85% in the capital, Port-au-Prince. Walking through downtown Port-au-Prince's boulevards is a lot like walking through a yard sale in American suburbia. Everywhere you look you see second-hand clothes, and piles of old shoes and leather belts. These items, used and thrown away by consumers in the US, are what constitute the majority of the informal economy in Haiti. They undercut local products and cause tailors and shoemakers to lose their livelihoods. These now unemployed skilled craftspeople find themselves peddling lower quality products. What the informal economy in Haiti has really become is a vicious cycle – the very items keeping the unemployed alive through informal labour cost them their jobs in the first place.

Table 6 Unemployment in Latin America

| Unemployment | 1997 | 1999 |
|---|---|---|
| Venezuela | 11.8 | 22 |
| Colombia | 12.4 | 19.7 |
| Argentina | 16.3 | 15.6 |
| Panama | 15.3 | 14.1 |
| Uruguay | 11.6 | 12.5 |
| Peru | 8.4 | 9.8 |
| Chile | 6.1 | 9.5 |
| Brazil | 5.6 | 7.8 |
| Regional Average | 7.2 | 9.3 |

But perhaps the first question should be why are the streets of Haiti filled with used American goods? Plans to make Haiti the Taiwan of the Caribbean began in the 1980's, and money was loaned on the condition that it be used to set up export-oriented industries, linking Haiti more closely with the international economy. Today these industries are championed as the saviour of the economy. They have added 40,000 jobs in the last five years, but there is a 70% unemployment rate and a population of eight million. This is part of the larger problem which includes the dumping of used American goods on the Haitian market. It also explains the growth of the informal economy as the only means of survival in Port-au-Prince and throughout the country. It causes massive migrations of people from rural areas to urban centres in search of jobs and the consequent overcrowding of the worst slums in the world. It helps us understand the virtual lack of social spending by the Haitian government by way of external debt servicing.

The nature of the IMF's work can be seen in Haiti and the results of its policies are crystal clear. The lowering of import tariffs, a strategy to make the export-oriented industries of Haiti more profitable (as most of them are owned by US corporations) and to create a market for used foreign goods have been the immediate and absolute cause of Haiti's rising unemployment rate, the growth of the informal sector and the loss of food security. Haiti has the lowest import tariff in the hemisphere at 3%, and also the lowest rate of food security in the world. Policies ignore the rural sector, forcing people to migrate. This creates a larger and more desperate work force which arrives in cities where there are too few precious jobs at US company sweatshops.

At the same time, programs of privatisation push ahead. Consequences on labour rights are ignored, and the informal economy is institutionalised through credit programs. These are the defining features of the neo-liberal economic and structural adjustment policies the IMF is imposing in Haiti.

## Corporate welfare in Haiti

(Edited from McGowan, 1998b)

Haiti, having the lowest wages in the entire Western Hemisphere, offers a very enticing environment to corporations intending to set up plants overseas. Such US companies as JCPenney, Disney, and Sears search for Third World countries characterised by high unemployment and poverty. In addition, they seek out those governments which have weak labour ministries, offer financial incentives, and are willing to meet the demands of corporations for infrastructure. Such concessions granted by the host government are called corporate welfare. Whereas corporations receive vast incentives to set up plants in Haiti, and, in the case of Disney, can even afford to pay their top CEO US$97,000 an hour, returns to the Haitian economy are minimal, and working and living standards of Haitian people, whose wages are generally below the minimum of 30 cents an hour, steadily decline.

How is it that exploitation of workers and preferential treatment of investors became the norm in Haiti (and elsewhere)? In order to discuss the complex answers to this question, it is necessary to first emphasise that the realities of (usually Third World) worker exploitation for the benefit of the few is not a naturally-occurring phenomenon: rather, it has been created through a complex and historically-grounded process of supplanting local production of the host country with imports, keeping wages low, and operating under a lack of regulation. In Haiti, this process involves the US and Haitian governments, multinational corporations, Haitian élites, and international financial institutions (IFIs), such as the World Bank and the IMF.

For over a decade, the World Bank and IMF have insisted on a low-wage strategy as a means of attracting foreign investment and have both designed and supported policies which restrict wages. In the early 1980s, the World Bank proposed a strategy to develop the export potential of both agro-industry and the country's maquila industry, where imported parts are assembled and exported. The agricultural projects involved marginal hillside lands being planted with coffee or cacao, and large tracts of flat and potentially more productive land being re-oriented toward the production of other export crops. Displaced peasants would flock to Port-au-Prince, forming a large labour pool for maquila industries. At the same time, new trade regulations, tax holidays, credit funds, technical assistance projects, and improved infrastructure were established to support the maquila sector, already aided by the continued suppression of worker rights and wages. This narrow strategy to increase Haiti's exports and tie its economy to the US market was quite successful. By 1985, for instance, the maquila sub-sector generated more than half of the country's industrial exports and earned one-quarter of its foreign exchange.

The World Bank and IMF's broader strategy of using foreign investment and exports as an engine for development, however, was an unmitigated failure. Throughout the 1980s, food production continued to decline, private investment consisted almost exclusively of residential construction, the assembly sector remained stagnant, and the value of agricultural exports dropped due to falls in the international price of coffee. The purchasing power of wages in 1985 was less than in 1970. Moreover, the value added from assembly-industry exports is very small: for instance, in 1989 apparel exports were worth a real value of only US $23.1 million, according to the US Commerce Department. This is due to the fact that goods to be assembled were shipped from the US, pieced together, and shipped out again, and few, if any, Haitian goods were used in the process. In addition, much of the tax-free profits made from the assembly sector are repatriated by US investors, not reinvested in Haiti.

Real wages in Haiti were halved during the decade of the 1980s, reaching US 25 cents an hour without benefits in 1989. A full-time minimum wage salary provided less than sixty percent of a family's basic needs (food, shelter, education) in Port-au-Prince.

The election of a populist government in 1990 brought with it opportunities for addressing the root causes of poverty never before seen in Haiti. Soon after taking office, Jean-Bertrand Aristide's administration made three proposals for economic reform designed to benefit the poor: the imposition of price controls on basic foodstuffs; raising the hourly minimum wage to a combined cash and benefit total of US$0.75 per hour; and the enforced payment of legally required social security taxes. Aristide also made major strides in improving government efficiency and structures, which drew pledges of US$511 million in grants and concessionary loans from the IFIs, USAID, and other bilateral and multilateral donors. However, despite new realities and opportunities, donors conditioned development assistance on the adoption of the same old structural adjustment policies, which included maintaining poverty-level wages, further opening of the Haitian economy, and stepped-up incentives to the export sector.

Submitting to structural adjustment conditionality was again the quid pro quo for US support for Aristide's return to Haiti after three years of bloody and destructive rule by a military junta between 1991 and 1994. And once again, wage restraint was a condition for receiving IFI support. In 1995, the IMF happily noted that the legal minimum wage established in June 1995 of 36 *gourdes* in reality 'falls well short of the real and US dollar equivalent minimum wage of ten years ago, and should not affect the good prospects for the export sector.' But, because the Haiti Labour Code mandated wage increases to keep up with inflation, the IMF wanted to take no chances: it provided part of the technical assistance to the Haitian government to revise the Labour Code to support the low-wage strategy of the IFIs. The IMF also

**Poorer health**

Studies are not conclusive regarding the impact of structural adjustment on health in Latin America and the Caribbean. However, growing inequalities in nutrition and health standards, even when averages may not have declined, are observed. The 1990s re-emergence of cholera and tuberculosis, for example, does not bode well for poorer population groups.

mandated a three-year government wage bill freeze. This meant that in order to increase the wages of its teachers, nurses, and other state employees, large numbers of people had first to be fired, so that the total wage bill was not increased. Such a strategy pits worker against worker and severely and deliberately undermines workers' rights of association and collective bargaining.

In contrast to the labour-busting IFI policies, investors benefit greatly from a whole range of subsidies promoted and supported by the IFIs. Under the current IMF program, tax holidays would be maintained for a period of 5-10 years. Under the agreement, the government is committed to 'assist the assembly industry to stay competitive by ensuring adequate electrical supply.' Toward this end, the Government of Haiti (GOH) will invest US$73 million from the Inter-American Development Bank (IDB) and the European Investment Bank in electrical plant, hardware, and repairs. In addition, as part of its loan agreements with the Bank and Fund, the GOH has reduced the telephone, electricity and customs fees, and tax incentives for foreign investors. At the same time, the government has removed food and fuel subsidies for the Haitian poor and increased their utility fees.

## Redefining security

Drugs, trafficking in women and children for prostitution, arms sales and money laundering are also enhanced by globalisation. Despite impressive advances in the 20$^{th}$ century, the world today faces grave privation and inequality within and among countries. Poverty is endemic and global. More than a quarter of the South's people do not achieve the minimal standards of human wellbeing – a life expectancy of greater than 40 years, access to education and other public services:

- 1.3 billion people have no potable water
- 1 in 7 school age children receive no education
- 840 million people are malnourished
- 1.3 billion people live on less than a US$1 per day.

The UNDP has defined the concept of 'human security,' which implies that people can exercise options with safety and freedom and the security that these options will be available to them in the future. It further elaborates that there are seven categories of human security (insecurity): economic, nutrition, health, personal, environmental, cultural and political. When human security is threatened anywhere it affects the whole world. Famine, ethnic conflicts, terrorism, pollution and drug trafficking do not respect national borders any more than do capital flows.

## The feminisation of poverty

The distribution of the burdens of structural adjustment has been unequal within households. Daily survival has been organised at the micro level, in every household. Throughout Latin America and the Caribbean there was a 'privatisation of the struggle for survival' (Berneria, 1996). Although there have been important collective initiatives as well, such as soup kitchens in Peru and Bolivia, the family has played the major role in daily survival. Berneria proposes that survival strategies can be summarised around three main areas: a) labour market adjustments, b) family budget adjustments, and c) restructuring of daily life. Each of these have specific gender dimensions and ramifications.

The task of caring for children, the sick , the elderly, and indeed the rest of us, is a daily responsibility mostly attended to by women in their households – referred to as 'social reproduction.' The 1995 UNDP *Human Development Report* calculated that women devote two thirds of their work time to non-remunerative activities geared toward taking care of others (men dedicate only one fourth of their time, on average, to such endeavours). This represents many hours of usually physically demanding work. Women also represent a disproportionate percentage of those in the service sectors, such as teaching and nursing, which pay considerably less than other professions with similar educational and aptitude requirements. Moreover, globalisation has reinforced these tendencies such that salary differences among sectors are increasing – with the service sectors ever more at the bottom of the heap.

Many empirical studies now allow us to better understand what happens. A study covering 165 countries, conducted from 1985 to 1990, concluded that more free trade increased women's participation in the paid workforce. A closer analysis showed that companies producing for export especially hire more women. But greater participation does not mean more equality or less discrimination, since women represent a disproportionate percentage of those hired or sub-contracted informally, with low salaries and few if any benefits. In competitive international markets, availability of such work is highly volatile and exploitative.

At the same time, social services which helped women with their social reproduction efforts have been drastically cut due to fewer government coffers and structural adjustment programmes.

Children and teens have also been affected by labour force strategies. Despite indicators which show a gradual improvement in education indices, this has not been the case for specific population groups for whom labour market participation has meant the interruption of schooling or lower attendance, which is likely to have effects on a whole generation. Primary school attendance drops have been mostly among girls who are often expected to stay home to care for domestic chores when their mothers have had to find a paying job, of whatever kind.

Adjustments in family budgets have resulted in less consumption of many goods, with food now consuming an inordinate percentage of income (world wide, the UNDP estimates it can be as high as 80%). Budget adjustments also led to the restructuring of daily life. Adjustment resulted in an increase in household chores, most of which fall upon women. Over the years, and now decades of adjustment, women organised on issues facing daily needs. The emergence of popular women's organisations has been an important part of the new social movements in Latin America and the Caribbean since the 1980s, resulting in the politicisation of daily life and a greater appreciation of gender issues. It is not surprising that at the 4th UN Conference on Women in Beijing in 1995, SAPSs were denounced as the main source of hardsh[...] for women and their families.

An unequal distribution of the burdens of adjustment has resulted in gender, age and class biases. A fourth bias, race and ethnicity, also needs to be highlighted. To the extent that indigenous and black people are disproportionately poor, there is also an implicit adjustment bias in these regards.

Ignored in most discussions of the IMF are the impact its policies have on virtually every aspect of women's daily lives, from their wages to their access to and quality of health, education and other services, to what they produce and consume, to how they use their own labour and to the economic struggles they face and the options they have for overcoming them. Extensive data from around the world shows that IMF/World Bank-imposed austerity and economic-reform programmes have stripped many women of what meagre health and education benefits were once available to them. Women's formal sector unemployment has increased due to IMF-induced recessions, privatisation, and government cutbacks. The proportion of female-maintained households continues to grow as men become unemployed or are pushed out of their traditional income-generating roles. Since the onset of SAPs, women have had to work harder and harder just to survive, shouldering enormous physical and psychological burdens.

Macro-economic policies can be devastating to women in a number of ways. By making credit prohibitively expensive, high interest rates diminish women's already scarce access to credit needed for production and household emergencies. Women workers are subject to massive layoffs both because they predominate in small and medium sized enterprises hardest hit by high interest rates and overall economic slowdowns, and because of the widespread practice of laying off women before men in both public and private sector operations. IMF-mandated low wages affect women directly, and have a ripple effect throughout the economy, placing further downward pressure on women's income.

Separate IMF policies often work at cross purposes. Measures against inflation are directly countered by devaluation, which increases the price on imports such as food, fuel, fertiliser and other productive inputs and has a negative impact on production, which increases the scarcity of goods, and makes prices rise even more. Because the IMF does not sufficiently desegregate inflation rates by categories of goods and services, situations such as those faced by women in Haiti are not uncommon. In that country, the IMF justifies its draconian policies by pointing to its success in decreasing inflation rates from 60% to 30%. Women, however, report price increases of one and two hundred percent on the imported food and medicines they need to survive. ·

...istence on 'labour market flexibility', a euphemism for
...ear the brunt of economic change, has directly and indirectly
...tatus of women workers. Not only are women being targeted
...d above, but such
...ve been able to
...g wages and status
within the workplace, which came
about only as a result of years of
struggle and organising within
unions, are now being wiped out
in the name of economic crises. In
addition, the deregulation of
labour markets has led to a
significant increase in part-time
and unstable employment and in
contracting-out arrangements,
where women undertake
piecework in their homes. Not only

| Third World countries<br>- some key facts |
| --- |
| 75% of the world's population |
| 20% of military expenditure |
| 17% of gross world product |
| 15% of global energy consumption |
| 11% of world education expenditure |
| 8% of the world's industries |
| 6% of global health expenditure |
| 5% of 'modern' technology |
| Iriarte, 1999 |

are women paid abysmally low wages for long hours, but, because regulation
is non-existent and there is no separation between living and work space,
women and their families face increased health hazards. The IMF choice to
undermine labour rights in the name of economic reform is a choice to
support and encourage the exploitation of women workers.

'For tens of millions of women around the world, IMF policies have
meant deprivation, uncertainty, and a never-ending struggle to survive.
Increases in violence against women due to higher levels of frustration and
stress within the family, caused by reduced income and intense financial
pressures brought on by SAPs, are reported around the world. The effects of
the mental stress of balancing multiple roles, the physical wear and tear of
overwork, and the psychological impact of grinding poverty and worry about
survival accumulate and damage women's health over the long term. Women's
own quality of life is damaged, as is their capacity for productive activity, for
ensuring the survival of their families, and for contributing to the viability
of their societies' (McGowan, 1998a).

These statistics demonstrate the minimal participation of Third World
countries in the world economy. With only one fourth of the world's
population, the Northern countries enjoy 83% of gross world product, 92%
of industrial investment, 94% of health care costs, 84% of energy use, 89%
of education expenditure, 95% of technological investment and 80% of
world arms production.

## Aid vs. debt relief

(Excerpted from Watkins, 1997)

Proponents of debt relief are quick to add that these monetary write-offs should not replace, but rather be additional to, official development assistance (ODA), whether bi- or multilateral. However, ODA had fallen to its lowest levels in 25 years at the end of the 20th century, by some 21% in inflation-adjusted terms between 1992-97 alone. Whether as a result of aid fatigue, the end of the Cold War and new geo-political interests, previous failures and waste, rampant corruption, racism, and/or pure disinterest or other causes, aid has fallen to its lowest level since targets were first set. In 1996, the OECD countries and G-7 agreed to provide 0.07 % of their GNP to development assistance in order to reduce the number of poor people globally by half by 2015.These targets were established at the Copenhagen World Summit for Social Development held that year.  By 1998, only Denmark, Norway, the Netherlands and Sweden came close and all other Northern donors weren't even half way to the target. To reach the target, Hanlon calculates that annually US$12 billion more in aid is needed for the poorest 28 countries, plus debt relief of US$75 billion annually.

This may seem like a lot of money, but annually US$800 billion is spent on military expenditures and US$400 billion on uncontrolled illicit drug trafficking. Hanlon and others believe that a well designed and funded debt relief strategy could provide both the incentive and sustained flow of resources needed to strengthen poverty reduction programs by releasing resources for investment in basic services such as health, education and rural infrastructure. So far, Uganda is the only country that easily comes to mind where this seems to be happening.

Net transfers of the World Bank to developing countries reached a peak of around US$5 billion in 1985. During the 1990s they have averaged less than US$2 billion. Concessional loans to the poorest countries have barely maintained their real value. The IMF has been a net *receiver* of financial resources from Southern debtors, including some of the poorest among them. Another problem with the IMF is that its record lending to Mexico and Russia after their crises in the 1990s strained the Fund's own liquidity to its lowest in history. Most ODA is a cruel hoax with net negative transfers from South to North and dependency-reinforcing mechanisms.

New commitments of export credits to developing countries doubled between 1990 and 1995 to US$80 billion. Yet sub-Saharan Africa, the region in which access to imports is most constrained, is being bypassed by the most important source: financial transfers. In 1994, the entire region received FDI worth the equivalent of flows to New Zealand alone. As a result, the

singly dependent on concessional aid flows, which in contrast
stment flows are in decline. In real terms aid has fallen by 3%
een 1993 and 2000. In 1995, net flows of ODA fell to their
a percentage of donor GNP since 1973. Meanwhile, the region's
are of world markets has cost it the equivalent of US$60 billion
per year over the last fifteen years. To put this figure in context, it represents
around three times the flow of development assistance received by African
governments.

Table 7   ODA (billions of US$) UNDP

|            | 1988 | 1993 | 1994 | 1995 | 1996 | 1997 |
|------------|------|------|------|------|------|------|
| net aid    | 48   | 56   | 60   | 60   | 58   | 50   |
| bilateral  | 37   | 39   | 41   | 41   | 39   | 32   |
| multi-lateral | 11 | 17   | 19   | 19   | 19   | 18   |
| % to LDCs  | 28   | 27   | 27   | 28   | 24   | 27   |

(most of the rest goes to China, Egypt and Israel)

## Don't be fooled by debt relief... it's just another way of reshaping the third world to the demands of capital

by John Pilger,  Jubilee South,  January 2000

The recent announcement by the British government that it is to 'cancel
third world debt' was a propaganda triumph. What a joy, sang the Guardian.
Debt forgiveness, said Bob Geldof, was an 'instinct' that was 'deeply rooted'
in Tony Blair's background. A code word in Gordon Brown's statement ought
to have been enough to alert even the gullible. Brown said that poor countries
would have their debt forgiven if they used the relief 'productively'. Later, he
wrote, 'both the IMF and the World Bank will show how together macro-
economic, structural reform and anti-poverty programmes can bring less
poverty and more growth.'

Not a single example exists where 'macro-economic, structural reform' –
he means laissez-faire capitalism imposed by the IMF and World Bank – has
alleviated mass poverty. Throughout the developing world, especially Africa,
structural adjustment programmes have destroyed jobs and public services,
while shaping local economies to the demand of transnational capital. In the
IMF's most 'successful' countries in sub-Saharan Africa, 13 children die every

92

minute from the likes of diarrhoea and malnutrition. Far from changing this, Brown's 'initiative' will reinforce it. To qualify, those countries that have been bled by British banks for 20 years will have to adhere to the 'conditionality' of the World Bank's 'Poverty Reduction and Growth Facility', which allows limited relief to highly-visible projects in countries that have been awarded World Bank/IMF brownie points for privatising and slashing jobs and services. The British Treasury will now have a fine excuse for not increasing Britain's scandalously mean aid programme.

There is a related hidden agenda here. This is the emergence, in another guise, of the discredited Multilateral Agreement on Investment (MAI). Had it not been for an international campaign against MAI, the 'Paris club' of rich governments, notably the Blair regime, would have signed away, in effect, the sovereignty and independence of developing countries to transnational capital: for the power to override national environmental and employment laws was at the core of MAI. The campaign against it forced governments, notably the French, to break ranks. MAI died. Or so it seemed.

Those who follow the chameleon enthusiasms of Clare Short, Blair's Secretary of State for International Development and defender of globalisation and illegal bombing, will note her latest: 'untying' of British aid from trade deals with British companies. Her stated reasons seem so sensible. Why should poor countries, she says, be restricted to British commercial contracts? Surely that is 'unfair'? What she omits to say is that the Blair government is at the forefront of 'liberalising' the entire procurement and contracting system in the third world: booty worth three trillion dollars, more than international trade. This 'untying' will allow British and other rich-world transnational corporations eventually to secure contracts in domestic markets previously barred to them. By comparison, the 14 per cent of the British aid budget presently exploited by British companies is chicken feed. This was not debated at Seattle, and there is the danger of a behind-closed-doors fait accompli.

In Britain, one of the obstacles to mounting an opposition to this is the compliance of leading voluntary agencies, or non-government organisations. The euphoria of certain NGOs following Gordon Brown's 'debt relief' announcement comes after a long seduction. NGOs represent the 'civil society' courted by new Labour. Having become dependent on government funding and gone some of the way with the fakery of 'productivity' linked to poverty relief, and having in recent years restructured their organisations right down to the use of claptrap market jargon, the more ambitious in the NGOs are in danger of slipping into bed with new Labour, the government of business. A few, such as Action Aid, remain unseduced, and there are those who clearly have serious doubts: witness the report by Louise Jury and

93

Matthew Lockwood, *Millennium Lottery: who lives, who dies in an age of third world debt?* published last month [December 1999] by Christian Aid.

When Peter Mandelson and his co-author Roger Liddle outlined in their book one of the blueprints for new Labour, they identified Britain's 'economic strengths' as: transnational corporations, the aerospace industry (arms) and the pre-eminence of the City of London. The evidence is now irrefutable: new Labour is a major facilitator of capital and of the sinister changes planned for the world's economy as part of globalisation.

On the day Gordon Brown announced his 'debt relief', this overshadowed the news that the Commons International Development Committee had discovered that a quarter of all export credit guarantees to poor countries were for the sale of weapons. Five days later, at the climax of the Hamilton

Table 8  The human story so far

| Great Achievements | Frustrations and Setbacks |
| --- | --- |
| more democracy and respect for human rights | new forms of racism, xenophobia, ethnic discrimination |
| technological advances and overall economic growth | more world poverty and hunger; massive unemployment and migrations; unbridled consumerism |
| end of the Cold War | more arms trafficking and many low-intensity civil wars; ever more violent civil society and rampant corruption |
| higher life expectancies | the poor suffer endemic diseases such as tuberculosis, cholera, malaria and newer diseases such as AIDS are out of control |
| accelerated communications | new technologies are not available to all but are used to promote publicity campaigns in favour of the elite |
| greater access to education | cultural imperialism and privatisation of education; value shifts |
| environmental interests heightened | environmental destruction on the rise |

Table 9  Human development balance sheet 1990-1997

## World Progress

• In 1997, people in 84 countries enjoyed a life expectancy of greater than 70 years, in comparison with only 55 countries in 1990. In this same time period the percentage of people with access to clean water rose from 40 to 72%

• During 1990-1997 the level of adult literacy rose from 64 to 76% and primary and secondary school attendance rose 7%

• Despite rapid population growth during this period, food production rose 25%

• From 1990-1997 real per capita GNP rose at an average annual rate of 1%. Per capita consumption overall rose an average 2.4% during the period.

• Women's secondary school attendance rose from 36-61% during the decade and their involvement in recorded economic activity rose 6%.

• From 1990-1997, early childhood mortality dropped from 76 to 58/1000. The percentage of one year old children immunised rose from 70% to 89%

• Between 1990-1997 highly polluting fuel use was reduced by 40% Between two thirds and three fourths of the world's Southern population live under relatively pluralistic and democratic regimes.

From UNDP Report, 1999

## World Privation

• During the 1990-1997 period people infected with HIV/AIDS doubled to more than 33 million. More than 1.5 billion people will not live to be 60 years old. More than 880 million have no access to health care and 2.6 billion have no access to basic sanitation facilities.

• In 1997 there were still 850 million adult illiterates. More than 260 million school age children receive no education whatsoever.

• 840 million people are malnourished. The food consumption of the richest 20% of the world's population is 16 times greater than the poorest 20%

• Nearly 1.3 billion people live on less than a US$1/day and nearly 1 billion can not meet their basic human needs. The richest 20% of the world's population 'earn' 74 times more than the poorest 20%

• An estimated 340 million women will not live to be 40.

• Between a quarter and a half of all women world wide have suffered physical abuse from a partner or relative.

• There are about 160 million malnourished children.

• There are more than 250 million children who work.

• Nearly 3 million people die from air pollution and more than 5 million die from contaminated water ingestion per year.

• At the end of 1997 there were more than 12 million refugees world wide.

and Fayed libel circus, the Trade Secretary, Stephen Byers, approved export credit guarantees worth £200 million to finance the huge Ilisu dam in Turkey that will assist in the ethnic cleansing of thousands of Kurds from their cultural heartland. No one wants it, apart from the repressive regime in Turkey, an arms client of the Blair government, and the British construction firm, Balfour Beatty, which stands to make a fortune. Does all this sound familiar? Recognise the name of the company from the Pergau Dam scandal in Malaysia, the epitome of Tory corruption? Little has changed, and we ought not to be fooled a second time.

## Thoughts on development

(Excerpted from Esteva and Prakash, 1998a)

From the outset, the 1980s looked like the lost development decade that it turned out to be. The 1990s ushered in the era of re-development, in the South, re-development means dismantling or destroying what was left by the 1980s' 'adjustment process,' in order to make room for the latest leftovers from the North (hazardous waste, obsolete or polluting technologies, unsaleable or forbidden commodities, etc.), for the maquilas (those fragmented and provisional pseudo-factories the North will maintain during this transitional period), and for ultra-modern transnationalized enclaves. ... Re-development in the South also means the economic colonialization of the so-called 'informal sector,' a massive assault on all forms of resistance to development. Today, re-development is tinted green. The growing concern with ecological destruction, which originally included a radical critique of industrial society, has been progressively recycled. In the name of a reasonably green 'common future,' 'sustainable development' has become the motto of the day – to sustain development itself, rather than to sustain nature or culture. Ecology operates increasingly as a cosmetic cover to protect – instead of prevent – the continuation of damaging processes.

'Basic needs' and 'popular participation,' like other 1970s novelties, get a new lease on life as

**Billionaires**

Throughout Latin America the number of billionaires rose significantly during the 1990s. In 1987 there were 6 throughout the entire region; in 1990 there were 8; in 1991 there were 20 and by 1994 this number had more than doubled to 41. At the turn of the 21st century, there are more billionaires in Latin America than there were in the world in 1987. In 1999, Europe had 36, Japan and Asia 40, the US 49 and Africa/the Middle East 8.

developers promise protection against the social short-sightedness of economic growth and anti-populist and anti-statist measures defined by globalization.

The Washington Consensus and the pragmatic policies often called neoliberalism are the latest substitute for... US hegemony now that the Cold War is over and only one Superpower remains....

As an unexpected side-effect of the four 'development decades,' most people on earth were assigned a new social category. Perceived only by exclusion, shovelled into the economy that is *not* public or private, they constitute the segment of the population that is *not* unionized, *not* formal, *not* with social security, *not* employed, *not* legal, *not* in the national accounts, *not* taxpayers, *not* a social class. They are always a residual category in both theory and politics. In the 1950s they were described in Latin America with the vague notion of marginality. In the 1970s [...] informality substituted it; but both were used as synonyms or equivalents. [...] In the 1980s popular participation became the clarion call [...] The 'new social movements' of the 1990s de-emphasized the struggle for state power, seeming to be looking instead for their share of economic or political benefits of development and more autonomy. Few seemed to be aware of the insurmountable contradictions between these two purposes. They tend to express their claims in the form of *human rights*, a process through which they assimilated the various imposed definitions of reality by the proponents of development.

The new development ethos emerging with the 1990s followed globalization [which] became the universal catechism of governments, political parties, and international institutions. Celebrated as the end of history, the new credo seemed to define the one and only path for the whole world in the 21$^{st}$ century.

## The benefits of being far from globalisation

*Los Tiempos*, Cochabamba, November 28 1999

In contrast to the agro-industrial sector, Bolivian peasants who still survive by bartering their products, in large measure have not felt the international economic crisis. 'We survive on our produce and not the international market,' explained a peasant leader, laughing. Globalisation is not feared in his community. Felipe Caseres, the Secretary General of Bolivia's United Confederation of Peasant Workers Union (CSUTCB), explained that there are two totally different Bolivias: one is tied to international market fluctuations, and another which is dedicated to traditional communal systems but receives no government assistance. Some agricultural sector experts think this phenomenon should be studied to determine how a communal approach could avoid the effects of fluctuations and crises in the international market. 'The only thing that affects me are natural phenomena like the weather – other than that I have no problems,' declared Marcelino Chambi from the province of Aroma. Quipse explained that traditional barter, *ayni* (communal lands), *mink'a* (communal work brigades), and other communal experiences have permitted the traditional agricultural sector to be less

Table 10 Developing Countries highest and lowest on the Human Development Index

| Five highest | Five lowest |
|---|---|
| Barbados | Central African Republic |
| Trinidad & Tobago | Ethiopia |
| Uruguay | Sierra Leone |
| Costa Rica | Burkina Faso |
| Cuba | Niger |
| (all LAC) | (all SSA) |

From UNDP Report, 1999

affected by the world crisis than agro-industry, where losses have been considerable. In different regions of the country and according to their products, peasants barter their respective products according to their basic values. Now, some large commercial companies are doing something similar. According to the magazine *New Economy* low sales obliged some business sectors to trade both services and products.

## Trade liberalisation, poverty and distribution: NAFTA and the case of Mexican agriculture

(Edited from Watkins, 1997)

The losers from free trade (are)…the producers of maize (corn), the country's staple food. Maize accounts for around half of Mexico's agricultural land area – and maize production occupies a pivotal position in maintaining rural livelihoods, generating income, and ensuring food supplies. Most smallholders are net-deficit households, selling maize in the post-harvest period and carrying out wage work to buy it after household supplies have run out. The vast majority of Mexico's maize farmers are operating on poor land, with limited access to credit, inputs, and equipment. Yields in rain-fed areas average around one fifth of the average for the US midwest, against which the maize sector is required to compete as trade restrictions are withdrawn. Estimates of the number of livelihoods lost in the maize sector as a consequence of trade liberalisation vary. According to one study, between 700,000 and 800,000 livelihoods are lost as maize prices fall, representing 15% of the economically active population in agriculture. This has profound implications for rural poverty and for regional inequality... Households will be forced into increasingly desperate survival strategies, including labour migration to commercial farm areas, to urban centres and to the US. There are important consequences for women. Research on the Tarascan plain of Michoacan has shown how male labour migration increased the workload on women and children. The withdrawal of children from schools in response to these pressures is one of the prime mechanisms for transmitting poverty across generations. It is estimated that women now comprise about one third of all the day labourers working in the Mexican countryside. To the extent that liberalisation accelerates these trends, it exacerbates problems of inequality and rural poverty. It is difficult to separate the effects of liberalisation from other factors, including the debt crisis of the 1980s and the financial crisis of 1994, when one million Mexicans lost their jobs while the number of Mexican billionaires* rose by 50%. Still disturbing trends emerge. Between 1989 and 1992, the richest 5% of the Mexican population increased their share of income from 24% to 29% of the total. Since 1992, the poorest half of the population has suffered a further decline in its share of national income.

99

# Chapter 7
# Environmental and political implications

## Growing debt

The same economic forces responsible for poverty are also responsible for extensive and growing environmental destruction. As the poor in the South pay their countries' illegitimate debts to their detriment, so too the price paid by the earth is environmental degradation. Economics is about the distribution and use of resources, all of which ultimately come to us from nature. An ecological perspective on the current world economic crisis shows the ways that the balance between humans and the rest of nature is being upset to the detriment of both. Southern indebtedness and world wide globalisation adversely affect the environment and people in several ways.

## The export imperative

Perhaps the main one is the export imperative. The current dominant paradigm calls for export-led growth to resolve the debt crisis, by bringing in foreign exchange. Because of the emphasis on promoting exports, particularly cash crop monoculture, many indebted Southern countries are forced to put even greater pressure on their already overstressed ecosystems by using often marginal land (e.g. cleared rainforest, which has very limited fertility) and petrochemical fertilisers and pesticides often outlawed in the North but imported and sold in the South by TNCs. Deserts are growing, with 2.4 million square kilometres now arid and another two million semiarid. Northeast Brazil, northern Venezuela, Argentina, Chile and the high plateaux of Peru and Bolivia are the most affected, with Central America, Haiti and Cuba close behind. Half the world's biodiversity is in Latin America but now some 10% of the world's species are under increasing threat of extinction. The need to increase short-term economic productivity is reducing the potential for long-term regenerative – sustainable – development.

Latin America is the most forested area remaining in the world, but it is indiscriminately cutting down its trees. Uncontrolled logging without adequate reforestation also abounds. The International Fund for Agricultural Development (IFAD), says that deforestation is occurring faster in Latin America than any other region of the world. Seven out of the ten countries in the world most responsible for deforestation are in the region and desertification and erosion are unfortunately keeping pace.

IRIARTE

On the other hand, the North consumes infinitely more than its share of resources. There would be no more trees left on the planet within two years if the whole world consumed as much paper as the US, which contains a mere 6% of the globe's population (Iriarte,1999). Strip mining, overfishing and petroleum extraction are examples of the many finite natural resources which are being exploited to death.

The neo-liberal myth of unlimited growth stands in acute contradiction to the reality of nature.

## The environment

(Edited from Bread for the World, 1996)

The World Bank and IMF together have more power to influence development in the Third World and Eastern Europe than any other institutions. The type of development that takes place does, and will continue to, change the lives of those it touches, and to dramatically alter local and global ecosystems.

IMF and World Bank practices have too often usurped local development priorities. Much of the Bank's US$22 billion annual lending supports projects and programs in environmentally sensitive areas, such as energy, agriculture and transport. The record of Bank lending in these areas has been needless environmental destruction and missed opportunities for more economically efficient and environmentally sound alternatives.

After a 1994 internal review found that between 1986 and 1993 15% of World Bank lending was directed to projects which were forcibly displacing 2 million people, the Bank closed or cancelled 22 of these projects, leaving 632,000 people to their fate. In addition, in FY 1994 the Bank approved 25 projects that will forcibly displace more people than in any other year in the Bank's history – 458,984. In contrast, in 1995 only 14% of the Bank's outstanding loan portfolio was directed towards the Bank-defined sectors of 'education' and 'population, health and nutrition'. Though continuing to offer new loans to projects requiring forced resettlement, the Bank can point to only a handful of projects in which the refugees it has created have not experienced a diminished standard of living.

The World Bank has a record of policies and programs that have often destroyed both the environment and the social fabric in country after country it claims to be helping. The Bank has failed spectacularly to achieve its stated goals of poverty reduction and 'sustainable development.' Furthermore, the World Bank's 'environmental' lending often serves as little more than camouflage for other, environmentally destructive projects.

101

Each relevant World Bank project and program, and each structural adjustment program of the IMF should ensure that it is consistent with protecting biodiversity and climate, and is in line with international environmental agreements, such as the one protecting the ozone layer. The World Bank and IMF should also incorporate into their planning and decision-making processes that value natural resources and ecosystems.

There should be a moratorium on World Bank funding for large dams until a) a comprehensive, locally driven river basin management plan is implemented that would guarantee that all appropriate alternatives for flood management, water supply, irrigation and power supply are exhausted before big dams are considered appropriate, b) a comprehensive review is carried out of past Bank lending for large dams, including impacts and performance, and a mechanism established to ensure that its findings are applied to future loan considerations and c) all conditions applying to the moratorium of projects involving forced resettlement are met.

Water projects should support conservation, demand-side management, improved efficiency in irrigation, the re-use of treated waste water, the transfer of 'clean' technologies to developing countries, and the extension of basic supply and sanitation coverage to populations not served. Energy lending should evaluate and support least-cost investments in end-use efficiency, conservation, and renewable energy sources. Investment decisions for transport lending should be based upon meeting basic mobility needs, especially for the poor, efficiently and at the least cost, using a variety of modes of transport. In all sectors, social and environmental costs should be fully integrated into the decision-making process.

Agricultural lending must be fundamentally redirected away from the current industrial agriculture model toward increasing support smallholder food production that builds on local knowledge and resources and increases local household and food security, local self-reliance and biophysical, social and economic sustainability. The World Bank should extend its commitment not to finance logging in primary moist tropical forests to all primary forests, including temperate and boreal forests. In addition, the World Bank should cease to support logging in an indirect fashion, such as through infrastructure and other development projects, as well as economic policies that accelerate forest exploitation.

## Cutbacks in public spending

Governments are responsible for enforcing environmental laws (where they exist) such as maintenance of wildlife preserves, safe water treatment and regulation of industrial and domestic pollution. But many of these programs have been significantly cut because of IMF austerity conditionalities to facilitate debt repayments. As described above in Chapter 4, international trade agreements also play a role. Southern sovereign debtors claims that the Northern creditors, especially the US, are trying to use environmental regulations as a protectionist ploy. 'A common concern expressed by Southern nations is that Northern countries, having higher standards of living and relatively high levels of environmental regulation already in place, use environmental and consumer protection as a cover for economic protectionism that limits Southern export markets. Rather than resorting to trade sanctions against poorer nations with limited regulatory infrastructure, the South maintains that the industrialised nations should aim to increase sustainable development in the South by providing easy access to environmental technology, funding for environmental protection and technical support' (Hunter and Van Dyke, 1999). But there remain legitimate ecological concerns. The impact of international trade on the environment was not a topic during the GATT Uruguay Round and was scheduled to be a side issue at the WTO Seattle meeting – NGOs and the US made it a central, though unresolved theme.

## The historic significance of Seattle

(Edited from Vandana Shiva, 1999)

The failure of the WTO meeting in Seattle was an historic watershed. First, it demonstrated that globalisation is not an inevitable phenomena (sic) which must be accepted at all costs but a political project which can be responded to politically. 50,000 citizens from all walks of life and all parts of the world were responding politically when they protested on the streets of Seattle for four days to ensure that there would be no new round of trade negotiations for accelerating and expanding the process of globalisation.

Trade Ministers from Asia, Africa, Latin America and the Caribbean were responding politically when they refused to join hands to provide support to a 'contrived' consensus since they had been excluded from the negotiations being undertaken in the 'green room' process behind closed doors. As long as the conditions of transparency, openness and participation were not ensured, developing countries would not be party to a consensus. This is a new context and will make bulldozing of decisions difficult in the future.

The rebellion on the streets and within the WTO has started a new democracy movement – with citizens from across the world and the governments of the South refusing to be bullied and excluded from decisions in which they have a rightful share.

Seattle had been chosen by the U.S to host the Third WTO Ministerial conference because it is the home of Boeing and Microsoft, and symbolises

103

the corporate power which WTO rules are designed to protect and expand. Yet the corporations were staying in the background, and proponents of free-trade were going out of their way to say that WTO was a 'member driven' institution controlled by governments who made democratic decisions. The refusal of Third World governments to rubber-stamp decisions from which they had been excluded has brought into the open and confirmed the non-transparent and anti-democratic processes by which WTO rules have been imposed on the Third World.

WTO has earned itself names such as World Tyranny Organisation because it enforces anti-people, anti-nature decisions to enable corporations to steal the world's harvests through secretive, undemocratic structures and processes. The WTO institutionalises forced trade not free trade. The WTO tyranny was apparent in Seattle both on the streets and inside the convention centre where the negotiations were taking place. Non-violent protesters including young people and old women, labour activists and environmental activists and even local residents were brutally beaten up, sprayed with tear gas, and arrested in hundreds.

The thousands of youth, farmers, workers and environmentalists who marched the streets of Seattle in peace and solidarity were outraged because they know how undemocratic the WTO is, how destructive its social and ecological impacts are, and how the rules are driven by the objectives of establishing corporate control over every dimension of our lives – our food, our health, our environment, our work and our future.

When labour joins hands with environmentalists, when farmers from the North and farmers from the South make a common commitment to say 'no' to genetically engineered crops, they are not acting in their special interests. They are defending the common interests and common rights of all people, everywhere. The divide and rule policy, which has attempted to put consumers against farmers, the North against the South, labour against environmentalists had failed. In their diversity, world citizens were united.

While the broad-based citizens campaigns stopped a new Millennium Round of WTO from being launched in Seattle, they did launch their own millennium round of democratisation of the global economy.

The real Millennium Round for the WTO is the beginning of a new democratic debate about the future of the earth and the future of its people. The centralised, undemocratic rules and structures of the WTO that are establishing global corporate rule based on monopolies and monocultures need to give way to an earth democracy supported by decentralisation and diversity. The rights of all species and the rights of all people must come before the rights of corporations to make limitless profits through limitless destruction.

104

Free trade is not leading to freedom. It is leading to slavery. Diverse life forms are being enslaved through patents on life, farmers are being enslaved into high-tech slavery, and countries are being enslaved into debt and dependence and destruction of their domestic economies.

We want a new millennium based on economic democracy not economic totalitarianism. The future is possible for humans and other species only if the principles of competition, organised greed, commodification of all life, monocultures, monopolies and centralised global corporate control of our daily lives enshrined in the WTO are replaced by the principles of protection of people and nature, the obligation of giving and sharing diversity, and the decentralisation and self-organisation enshrined in our diverse cultures and national constitutions.

A new threshold was crossed in Seattle – a watershed towards the creation of a global citizen-based and citizen-driven democratic order. The future of the World Trade Organisation will be shaped far more by what happened on the streets of Seattle and in the non-governmental organisation (NGO) events than by what happened at the WTO meeting.

The rules set by the WTO violate principles of human rights and ecological survival. They violate rules of justice and sustainability. They are rules of warfare against the people and the planet. Changing these rules is the most important democratic and human rights struggle of our times. It is a matter of survival.

Citizens went to Seattle with the slogan 'No new round, turnaround'. They have been successful in blocking a new round. The next challenge is to turn the rules of globalisation and free trade around, and make trade subservient to higher values of the protection of the earth and peoples' livelihoods.

The citizens' Seattle round of the democratisation of the food system synthesised common concerns of people from across the world to ensure that the way we produce, distribute, process and consume food is sustainable and equitable. In the Third World and the industrialised world, common principles have started to emerge from peoples' practices to ensure safe and healthy food supply. These principles enable us to shift to nature-centered and people-centered food systems.

1. Diversity rather than monocultures to ensure higher output per acre.

2. Decentralisation and localisation in place of centralisation and globalisation.

3. Ecological processes instead of industrial processes of farming.

4. Food rights and food security rather than free-trade as the basis of distribution.

5. Democratic control rather than corporate control of the food system.

6. Patent-free and genetic engineering free farming to ensure the respect and protection of all species and the integrity of ecosystems and cultures. This involves excluding life forms from TRIPS and Biosafety from WTO rules of free trade.

7. Cultural diversity in place of the global monoculture of fast foods and industrial food chains.

8. Small farms and small farmers in place of corporate farms and absentee land owners. This involves protection of existing small farms and land reforms to redistribute land.

9. Fair trade, not free trade, to ensure farmers and producers get a fair return. Trade as a means rather than end, with global trade subservient to values of ecological sustainability, health and social justice.

Against all odds, millions of people from across the world have been putting these principles into practice. The post-Seattle challenge is to change the global trade and national food and agricultural policies so that these practices can be nurtured and spread and ecological agriculture, which protects small farms and peasant livelihoods, and produces safe food, is not marginalised and criminalised. The time has come to reclaim the stolen harvest and celebrate the growing and giving of good food as the highest gift and the most revolutionary act.

## The expansion of transnationals

In addition to promoting export-lead economic policies, the BWIs also require debtor countries to open their doors to international investments. Driven by an unchecked profit motive and not accountable for their destructive activities (there are no applicable standards yet in place) TNCs foist ecologically unsound practices upon the South, ranging from agricultural projects to mineral mining and industrial pollution. TNCs maintain that under NAFTA and other trade agreements measures which fall under the area of protection for the environment constitute indirect expropriation of their assets because they allegedly reduce their anticipated profits.

'In Chile, the massive infusion of FDI into copper mining has resulted in the overproduction and oversupply of the red metal at the world level which led to a period of low international prices without historical precedent. This reduced the inflow of foreign exchange into the country after 1995, which grew worse after the Asian crisis. This massive investment in exploitation on non-renewable resources increased pressure on the ecosystem, producing multiple damages to the environment and surrounding communities' (Dillon, 1998).

Citizens world wide are increasingly aware of global institutions (like the WTO and the World Bank) and their harmful impacts on the environment and human rights. But other secretive, often overlooked government bodies known as export credit agencies also play a leading role in the process of corporate globalisation. Important issues of concern include their project impacts, their lack of transparency and consultation with civil society, and their failure to make progress in adopting internationally accepted environmental and social policies.

Export Credit Agencies and Investment Insurance Agencies, commonly known as ECAs, are public agencies that provide government-backed loans, guarantees and insurance to corporations which seek to do business overseas in developing countries and emerging markets. Most industrialised nations have at least one ECA, which is usually an official or quasi-official branch of their government. ECAs are now the world's biggest class of public finance institutions supporting private sector projects, collectively exceeding in size the World Bank Group.

Because of the inherent risks of controversial projects in the mining, forestry, oil and gas, coal, power sectors, many of these potentially harmful projects in the developing world could not go forward but for the support of bilateral ECAs. These ECAs provide the political and financial support that allows corporations to proceed with projects that harm the environment and disrupt the lives of the people in the affected regions.

## The challenge of social and environmental sustainability: the case of Export Credit Agencies (ECAs)

(Edited from Rich, 1998)                         432 billion exp.

In 1996, industrialised countries' ECAs supported US$432.2 billion worth of exports in developing countries (DCs). The amount equals 10% of all world trade, 24% of total indebtedness in DCs and 56% of government debts of DCs. This represents a far higher amount than all debt owed by DCs to multilateral development banks (MDBs).

Roughly US$100 billion per year are made available in the form of new ECA loans. Around half of this amount goes to projects which are not just debt-generating, but also have a considerable negative impact on the environment. Even the World Bank cannot get complete information on what ECAs are doing. There is a permeable barrier between the private sector and ECAs which means that private debt is often not as private as it looks. ECAs have financed grotesquely unsustainable projects, including arms exports. It can be seen therefore that public money from the North is working irrationally at cross-purposes: one the one hand, there are bilateral development agencies and MDBs; on the other hand there are ECAs (subsidised by governments), which finance projects the other two would not touch publicly.

International treaties on sustainable development and biodiversity are undermined by the activities of ECAs. An ECA that took the environment into account would lose its competitive position *vis à vis* other ECAs. The US Export-Import Bank turned down a project in China on environmental grounds, only to see the project picked up by other ECAs from Japan, Germany and Switzerland. This zero-sum-game does not encourage ECAs to apply standards to the projects they are financing.

NGO activity on ECAs has been especially strong in the call for the adoption of common environmental and social standards and civil society involvement in ECA projects, or at least better information, greater transparency and screening possibilities. These calls were greeted with incredulity by rich country ECAs.

It is important and NGOs should not only pin their hopes on having some global mechanism to oversee standards. The energy of NGOs can be dissipated by continuously chasing after new global institutions with the resources to keep them at bay. They forget that the members of these institutions are their own governments, which means there is a need to look at the collection of governments rather than the anonymous or remote bodies that somehow are not connected with their lives.

NGOs should not be looking for easy, global solutions but should be prepared to accept local, national and regional solutions which might look chaotic and not always work. However, this is better than having an imposed international regime which assumes a kind of uniformity and takes away more of the power from the state to engage in economic policy making.

## The IMF: selling the environment short

(Edited from Friends of the Earth, 2000)

The growing civil society movement coalescing around issues such as debt and sustainable development has led to a shift in the debate surrounding structural adjustment policies in the developing world. In much of this new thinking, however, there is a major missing element: the environment. For years, environmentalists around the world have been concerned about the impact of the IMF and World Bank's economic development approach on the global environment. While the World Bank instituted policies to incorporate environmental considerations in its project lending, it has not extended these policies to structural adjustment policy lending, which today represents more than half of its portfolio. The IMF claims to defer to the

World Bank on environmental matters, but promotes export-led development that has major environmental impacts without asking the World Bank for any formal assessment of the environmental implications of its approach. The World Bank has failed to provide environmental guidance to the IMF, and is even delinquent in assessing the environmental impacts of its own structural adjustment loans.

A recent internal World Bank study found that fewer than 20% of World Bank adjustment loans included any environmental assessment. Nor does the IMF require any written, public environmental analysis from the World Bank or other knowledgeable institutions. The IMF plays a critical role in setting countries' economic frameworks and indicating to other donors, such as the World Bank and bilateral donors, the health of a country's economy. Though the IMF is not an environmental institution, its role in setting economic stabilisation and structural adjustment policies means that it has a major impact on the environment. These impacts must be taken into account in advance of formulating country programmes. Washington DC-based Friends of the Earth released a report in early 2000 which is intended to provide a snapshot of how the IMF's economic policies have led to increased pressure on the environment and jeopardised the potential for sustainable development in various countries. The report looks at cases across the globe where the IMF's programmes have led to reductions in environmental spending, increases in natural resource exploitation and the weakening of environmental laws. The report identifies how the IMF's programmes affect the environment and why environmental issues need to be at the core of issues evaluated. The report concludes with a series of recommendations that the IMF and its member governments should institute in order to begin to rectify this problem.

The IMF and World Bank have claimed that structural adjustment is too complex to assess accurately. They assume that any policy changes will achieve economic stability and thereby promote sustainable development. While economic instability is admittedly a threat to sustainable development, the IMF's approach to economic reform has generally promoted and rewarded short-term monetary improvements in export performance and budget balances, and thereby encouraged unsustainable development. The result has been too many economic policies that promote environmental degradation and too few policies that promote positive environmental gains.

The IMF's economic policies affect the environment in various ways. One major goal of structural adjustment programs (SAPs) and stabilisation programs is to generate foreign exchange through a positive trade balance. To meet the IMF's ambitious targets for currency reserves and trade balance, countries must quickly generate foreign exchange, often turning to their

109

natural resource base. Countries often over-exploit their resources through unsustainable forestry, mining, and agricultural practices that generate pollution and environmental destruction, and ultimately threaten future exchange earnings. Exports of natural resources have increased at astonishing rates in many countries under IMF adjustment programmes, with no consideration of the environmental sustainability of this approach. Furthermore, the IMF's policies often promote price-sensitive raw resource exports, rather than finished products. Finished products would capture more value-added, employ more people in different enterprises, help diversify the economy, and disseminate more know-how.

Structural adjustment and stabilisation also aim to generate positive government budget balances. In the effort to rapidly trim budget deficits, governments are forced to make choices, and inevitably, the environment loses. Decreased spending weakens government ability to enforce environmental laws and diminishes efforts to promote conservation. In addition, governments are told to increase private investment and to reduce the role of the state in favour of private sector development. Budget priorities are often directed toward business promotion, creating a further strain on cash-strapped environmental enforcement agencies. Governments may also relax environmental regulation to meet SAP objectives of increasing foreign investment.

The other environmental tragedy of adjustment is that economic policies that could help promote environmental sustainability are being ignored. The IMF regularly advises countries on their tax policy: they could broaden their scope to emphasise ecological taxes. Ecological taxes would generate revenue and benefit the environment by discouraging wasteful and excessive natural resource use. Instead, the IMF currently favours a regressive value-added tax system. In the IMF's effort to build countries' accounting systems and statistics- tracking capabilities, it could also pursue environmental full-cost accounting to help countries and international financial institutions realise the value of natural resources to a country's economy, thereby encouraging sustainable resource use. Both of these areas, green taxes and environmental full-cost accounting, are within the IMF's technical assistance function, and would contribute to environmentally sustainable development.

Until policy makers recognise the importance of genuine sustainable economic development and the role the IMF plays, and take immediate steps to truly promote environmentally sustainable development in all their policies and programmes, global environmental degradation will continue and poverty will be perpetuated. Environmental protection and sustainable resource use must be considered a core component of any strategy aimed at economic policy reform and poverty alleviation.

## Waste dumping

(Dillon, 1998)

The latest environmental horror being perpetrated upon foreign-exchange starved debtor countries is the dumping of Northern hazardous wastes in the South. Several Caribbean nation islands have entered into hard currency deals to accept such 'garbage'. Adding insult to injury, 'US-based Metaclad, a waste disposal company, as one example, is seeking compensation from the Mexican government because the state of San Luis Potosi refused it permission for a waste disposal facility. The State Governor ordered the site closed down after a geological audit showed the facility would contaminate the local water supply. Metaclad has sought compensation of some US$90 million for expropriations and for violations of national treatment and prohibitions on performance requirements. (see Chapter 4 for more on these issues)

## Indigenous people

(Bello, 1994)

Often the poor are blamed for the South's deteriorating ecological plight since they are forced to use increasingly marginal plots to grow their subsistence crops as better lands are consumed by agricultural export production. An argument which sounds remarkably like blaming the victim. Overall in Latin America, beef production is up but domestic consumption is down since it is being produced for export. Not only does export beef production not feed the region's hungry, but it also takes away sustainable food alternatives from them by converting self-reliant agricultural land into export cattle pastures. The real culprits are the Northern IFIs which insist on export promotion and government spending slashes to service the South's debts and supply the wasteful lifestyles of elites in both the North and the South. 'Indeed, it is hard to see how structural adjustment can be made environment friendly, since it contributes to impoverishment and more inequality, which are two of the key causes of environmental degradation.

## Globalisation and suicide

(Edited from Campos, 1999)

One April night in 1995, Silvinha Cavalcante left her thatched shack in Dourados, Brazil and never returned. She crossed the open plains of her reservation where once there were dense forests, and stopped to contemplate a single guayabo tree. Her family searched for her and eventually found her hanging from that solitary tree. The Guarani Kaiowa girl was 12 years old when she died.

Suicide, something previously unheard of among Brazil's indigenous population, is now decimating aboriginal peoples in the remote frontier area of western Mato Grosso do Sul. Indigenous culture experts attribute this phenomenon to poverty, the related disintegration of the family and failure to adjust to the violent encroachment of white colonists, the worst destroyers of the environment. Cattlemen, farmers, gold miners, and timber cutters are leaving in their wake a terribly impressive desert.

Problems for the Guarani tribe began with the cutting down of their forests for cattle grazing and soybean cultivation. There were 9,065 indigenous people who lived in Dourados on 3,500 hectares of land, but the 'success' of the cattlemen and soy growers began to dramatically reduce the traditional hunting and fishing livelihoods of the Guarani.

Augusto Roa Bastos, writing about Paraguay, described how the forest people 'sang in agony about their own deaths.' Today, the Amazon basin not only represents the gasping lungs of the planet but also the survival of indigenous people and of the earth's greatest biodiversity. The Guaranis and other indigenous peoples feel entrapped by the arrival of 'civilisation' which for them symbolises nothing less than the barbarism of modernity. When they don't choose suicide they must migrate to urban centres where they are equally condemned to the edges of society.

This is one of the most nefarious results of globalisation – the direct or indirect extermination of ethnic minorities. Economic and political globalisation can only mean the loss of indigenous identity, subjecting them to the edges of one culture – that of the world market.

## Climate change

(Edited from from *Who Owes Who?* Christian Aid report, 1999)

> '1998 was the warmest on record and also the worst year on record for natural disasters.' *Financial Times*, 25 June 1999

What is debt? Rich countries pursue highly indebted poor countries to service their foreign financial debts, at great cost to the millions who subsequently go without vital health and education services. But industrialised countries are themselves responsible for a much larger debt to the global community. Their reckless use of fossil fuels has helped create the spectre of climate change – a storm cloud which hangs over everyone's future.

And it is poor people in poor countries who suffer first and worst from both extreme weather conditions connected to climate change, and from the struggle to service unpayable foreign debts. Our understanding of debt, and who owes it, is horribly wrong and needs changing.

Geological history shows the earth gripped by natural cycles of cooling and warming.

Whatever the distant future holds for our climate is hard to predict. But today, and looking forward through the next century, the lives and livelihoods of more than one billion people are threatened by the effects of global warming, increased by human activity. Many of those most at risk live in poor countries. By 2025 the UN estimate that over half of all people living in developing countries will be highly vulnerable to floods and storms. Already development work has been affected in many countries from Bangladesh to Tanzania and Honduras.

To solve the problem or, at least, mitigate its worst effects, we will all have to live within our environmental budget. The atmosphere can only absorb a certain amount of greenhouse gases before disruption begins. So, their emission needs controlling. As, each day, industrialised countries delay action on the 60-80 per cent cuts that are needed, they go over-budget and are running up an environmental or carbon debt. Ironically those same countries today stand in judgement over much poorer countries who have comparatively insignificant conventional, financial debts.

The real carbon debt is the accumulation of surplus carbon dioxide beyond the capacity of the environment to absorb. But, our illustrative estimates also show the G7 running up carbon debts in economic efficiency terms of around $13 trillion each year. On the same calculation the group of highly indebted poor countries (HIPCs) are running up credits of between $141-$612 billion because of their under-use of fossil fuel resources and the climate. At the higher end of the scale this gives a credit three times the conventional debt of the HIPCs, which stands around $200 billion. Not only does this question the continuing legitimacy of poor countries struggling to service debts which they cannot afford, it also points to the responsibility of the industrialised nations to reverse declining flows of resources and contribute far more toward sustainable development in developing countries.

With or without climate change and the carbon debts owed by rich countries, unpayable poor country debts should be cancelled, to achieve the global poverty reduction which the whole international community is committed to. Most of that community, through a series of international agreements, is also committed to controlling global warming and cancelling poor country debt. But, the carbon debt makes two points clear:

1. Rich countries' huge and growing debt to the global community for climate change removes the last shred of moral legitimacy to keep holding poor countries hostage to their own much smaller, but still unpayable, financial debts.

2. Responsibility for climate change, and ability to pay, means industrialised countries should commit significant new resources and technology to help poor countries affected by the increasingly volatile and uncertain global environment.

## Hurricane Mitch hits Honduras

(Edited from Hernandez and Rodgers, 1999)

Natural disasters are never just about the forces of nature: they have human causes and effects too. When Hurricane Mitch devastated Central America in October 1998, 15,000 people died and a million were left homeless in underdeveloped Honduras, the second poorest country in the Western hemisphere. What turned Mitch from a natural hazard into a human disaster was a chain reaction of social vulnerabilities created by long-term climate change, environmental degradation, poverty, social inequality, population pressure, rapid urbanisation and international debt.

Poverty is the most persistent cause and the most pernicious effect of human disaster. Hurricane Mitch plunged millions of people in Honduras into a life-or-death struggle with deepening poverty. It raised crime rates, pushed up domestic violence and drove up to a million people from their homes, because their farms or their jobs could no longer sustain them. Thousands of others were forced to return to environmentally unstable homes and fields because they were too poor to buy their way out.

Hurricane Mitch had two unexpected consequences say Honduran civil society organisations: it sparked an intense national debate on the need to rebuild the country's democratic institutions as well as its bridges. It also rekindled a global debate on the morality of international debt, and whether poor nations stricken by natural disaster should receive special help. Both these concerns were prominent at a major international conference in Stockholm in May 1999, where the international community pledged US$9 billion in post-Mitch aid to Central American countries – US$2.5 billion of it to Honduras. Goals and principles adopted in the conference declaration sought to reduce the region's social and ecological vulnerability and to transform its politics by promoting decentralisation and democratisation.

But democratic transition has a long and painful history in Central America. Natural disasters have a way of shaking up its politics but often not permanently. One year on, Honduras remains locked in a post-colonial plantation economy, where patronage politics rule, corruption is described as a chronic infirmity and the military still casts an ominous shadow. So far the country has received little of the US$2.5 billion pledged at Stockholm, reportedly because of continuing doubts about financial management. A poorer, more polarised Honduras will be even further away from the democratisation the Stockholm Declaration seeks.

Honduras' ecology as well as its politics will leave it deeply vulnerable for years to come. Commercial logging, peasant farmers pushed onto marginal lands and rapidly expanding urban slums on the hillsides surrounding its major cities, make the country a perennial prisoner of floods and landslides. A year after Mitch, seasonal rains killed 30 people and displaced thousands.

The principle of debt relief for poor states was agreed at the annual World Bank/International Monetary Fund meeting in September 1999. But it remains unclear who will benefit and how. Under the present agreement, Honduras will not qualify for debt relief for four more years, by which time it will owe another $2 billion in debt servicing – the same amount that the World Bank estimated that Mitch-related damage in the public sector would cost to rebuild. If we continue to give with one hand and take away with the other, Honduras is going to remain perpetually in debt to disaster.

Hurricane Mitch also has a global message and a universal relevance. Climate change and global warming are making the world more vulnerable to natural disaster. Poor people in vulnerable habitats will be exposed to higher levels of natural hazard. Mitch is a wake-up call, a portent of a larger deterioration in our biosphere. The poor will pay first and we will pay later. In a globalised world, poverty remains the greatest moral and practical problem of our time. We walk away from it at our peril.

## NAFTA and the environment

The tremendous increase in speculative financial flows, the surge in direct foreign investment and the volume of trade sparked by NAFTA are having a significant deleterious impact on the environment. The combined result of the far-reaching changes implemented following the signing of NAFTA has been a new period of free market activity. This has substantially polarised Mexican society and reorganised the geographic distribution of economic activity, placing mounting pressures on fragile ecosystems and unsustainable demands on land and water resources throughout the country. In addition to the troublesome growth of maquila plants along the border and other investments in the semiarid north, Mexican policymakers intensified their assault against peasants, transferring official maize subsidies from rain-fed regions to wealthier irrigated regions. Indeed, one of the most significant changes resulting from Mexico's reckless entrance into the global economy has been a marked deterioration in the material conditions of workers and peasants throughout the country. When the complex support system that had for so long shaped their way of life and patterns of economic activity was suddenly dismantled workers and peasants found themselves both without a means of income and, frequently, uprooted. Many people were forced to migrate, further reducing the quality of life as families were separated, and large portions of the national population began to engage in more marginal activities, with pronounced impacts on the environment. In other sectors, the side effect of these 'adjustment aftershocks' was a lack of human, material and financial resources; businesses and government were obliged to take shortcuts in environmental management chores or simply to postpone maintenance and investment in capital improvements, such as environmental infrastructure for toxic waste reduction and emission controls.

## Politics

As we saw in the previous chapter, the world economy is characterised by persistent poverty and widening inequalities at the national and international levels. If history provides one lesson, it is that poverty and inequality do not create a climate for political stability. One of the cruel and paradigmatic myths of globalisation is that it can and will eventually improve the lot of the majority. In reality, however, the current dominant export-led growth, neo-liberal 'development' model has created marginalisation, polarisation, and deepening social tensions. The symptoms of social decay are clearly visible in rising crime rates, drug abuse and civil violence of all sorts, fostering political extremism. 'To put it bluntly, we are on the road to anarchy and chaos – and we have been there before. In the 1930s, unregulated markets and the collapse of institutions resulted in economic crisis and fuelled the political tensions which led to a world war [... ] It is difficult to escape the conclusion that we are again headed for a descent into economic Darwinism. Inequalities between countries, and between people within countries have reached levels which, quite apart from undermining human welfare, threaten political stability' (Watkins, 1997). Economic forces are running ahead of political responses.

Latin American politics and its relation to market forces is significantly different at the turn of the 21st century than it was even a decade earlier when democracies in the region were still emerging, wars threatened much of Central America, terrorism reigned in Peru, debt riots were a common feature and US foreign policy was living out its lasts gasps of anticommunist paranoia. The post-Cold War decade of the 1990s was characterised by very different realities. From 1989-98 there were 61 armed conflicts in the region, three involving international disputes and the rest domestic civil unrest.

The 70 year-old reigning PRI political party in Mexico lost the mayoral election of the capital city to the leftist Party for Democratic Revolution (PRD) and the general elections to the National Advance Party (PAN) for the first time. With the dawn of NAFTA in 1994, the country woke to the Chiapas-based Zapatista popular movement and guerrilla against neoliberalism. That the sympathetic Zapatistas replaced the malevolent Peruvian Shining Path as the foremost insurgency in Latin America is telling (the Colombian struggle continues but is so entrenched and long-term that it is another story altogether). Civil wars in Guatemala, Nicaragua and El Salvador ended. So called 'populist' presidents (who many perceive as dictators in sheep's clothing) now rule in Venezuela and Peru; 17 year Chilean dictator Pinochet waited in British residential arrest for 18 months to see if he would be deported to Spain for crimes against humanity; an ex-military dictator, General Hugo Banzer, is the democratically-elected president of Bolivia. At the century's change, only Ecuador (see Chapter 5 above and below in this chapter) faced serious popular unrest as a result of neo-liberal economic policies. Now, corruption is emblematic and replacing the Cold War is the war on drugs, under the same old US influence.

## Democracy and neoliberalism

(Excerpted from Berneria and Dudley, 1996)

In the 1990s, the notion that stable democracy owes a great deal to a market economy was pervasive. The implications of this for democracy are significant. The ideal behind a rapid transformation toward democracy and market capitalism is that the former disperses political power and the latter economic resources in ways that reinforce one another. This does not seem to be the case in Latin American democracies undertaking economic liberalisation programs. These are *sui generis* democracies, which exhibit high levels of discretionary power in the hands of the executives.

For example, in Chile the ex-dictator stepped down from office, remained as head of the Army and senator for life, leaves an entirely new institutional

117

architecture in place, and gets the agreement of the whole party system, let alone the business community. In Peru an amateur politician is elected, dissolves Congress (and then packs the judiciary with his own cronies), drafts a new constitution and manages to get it passed by popular vote and has run for a third 5-year term when the previous Constitution allowed for only one.

In Argentina the president rules virtually by decree, appoints the Supreme Court and drafted a new constitution which in the process was open to compromise on everything except (not allowing) the re-election of the President.

Yet these regimes have been stable, in spite of the simultaneous implementation of potentially destabilising economic reforms. This highlights that much of the stability depends on new state-business relations forged in the last two decades. New firms emerged with increased structural power which gave them more direct access to government decision-making arenas at the expense of more institutionalised forms of representation – and of course labour. State-business relations have become the new 'coalitional fulcrum' of Latin American politics.

So we do not see much dispersion of power in the newly democratising nations of the region. We witness a more active political involvement of business, given its (greater) access to the state apparatus. The consequences of economic reforms have translated into a more concentrated, diversified and 'conglomerised' bourgeoisie which seems committed to not abdicate from politics anymore and thus leaves little room for the different forms of state autonomy of the past. This is the new ruling coalition which has, paradoxically, provided support to democracy – to this type of democracy. Neoliberal democracy seems to be the only game in town in Latin America today.

## Political implications of neo-liberal globalisation

(Edited from Woodward, 1998)

As well as the direct constraints they impose on economic policies, direct and equity investment have potentially important political dimensions. With very high rate of return on foreign direct investment, avoiding net foreign exchange outflows entails a very rapid increase in the stock of foreign investments. This in turn implies a commensurate increase in the role of TNCs in the economy. TNCs can thus be expected to acquire a major and increasing role in the political process to defend their commercial interests. Moreover, their resources and corporate experience in political lobbying will generally be considerably greater than that of domestic interest groups, particularly those representing non-commercial interests, or even political parties; and their influence will often be shared with other influential external agencies, such as the developed country governments and the IMF and the World Bank. There is a real risk that TNCs will thus exercise a disproportionate influence in the policy-making process, skewing policies further towards their interests and, within the constraints imposed by their need to maintain political stability, away from the interests of the population at large. This suggests at best a weakening of the democratic process, and in some circumstances may actually reinforce anti-democratic pressures.

The conservative Heritage Foundation in the US and the *Wall Street Journal* released their *Index of Economic Freedom 2000* report at the end of 1999, declaring Latin America to be the region of the world where neo-liberal policies had most advanced over the last three years. Most of the region's countries had reduced inflation (Argentina from a staggering 3,000% in 1989 to 1% in 1998). In their eyes, El Salvador is the new 'Hong Kong' of Latin America, and Chile has the most neo-liberal economic policies in the region. Since its civil war ended, El Salvador has opened its doors to foreign investment, mostly in cheap labour assembly factors – maquilas.

Bolivia is a good example of the general thesis of the *Index* – neo-liberal economic policies inevitably lead to greater growth. This was the first Latin American country, back in the mid-1980s, to adopt structural adjustment programmes bringing hyperinflation under control, cutting government spending and attracting some foreign capital (largely to buy privatised national enterprises). Corruption continues to be rampant, drug trafficking continues and it remains the poorest country in the region, but according to the *Index* this Andean country is a 'success'.

## Unrest in Ecuador

Entering a new millennium, there is no doubt that Ecuador is the most severely politically affected country in the region relative to the neo-liberal economic model. In early January 2000, the government declared a national state of emergency in light of increasing civil unrest concerning the economic crisis. The army was sent out into the streets to 'restore order, assure citizen safety and help maintain democracy.' The constitutional rights to gather, march and protest were suspended and some 50 people arrested. Civil society, led by a Patriotic Front, called for President Mahuad's resignation and the dissolution of both the Congress and Supreme Court. Schools were briefly closed and the health and transport sectors went on strike with a general national strike announced. The indigenous population was especially organised in these protests. Financial analysts and the business community publicly called for the President's resignation. Rumours of a possible military coup abounded.

Refusing to resign, President Mahuad nonetheless announced dramatic measures in light of the financial crisis where interest rates reached 80%, inflation 60%, and the minimum wage plummeted to the equivalent of US$4 a month. Ecuador's currency, the *sucre*, devalued more than 300% in the last half of 1999 and a staggering 55% in five days in early January 2000, reaching a wopping 28,000 sucres to US$1.

Finally, under IMF pressure, Mahuad agreed to 'dollarise' the sucre, privatise telecommunications, electric companies and social security, called for the resignation of his entire cabinet and agreed to resume Brady Bond payments in March. Mahuad also announced he would talk to the US before continuing further negotiations with the IMF, in open deference to the US's influence. President Clinton called President Mahuad to assure his backing and implying to the Ecuadorian public and army that the US would not look favourably upon a military coup. Ecuador, once considered the Switzerland of South America for its mountainous beauty and stability, bore little resemblance those days to its alpine counterpart.

The coup came on January 21 2000, but in a unique form. A tripartite coalition of military colonels, the ex-president of the Supreme Court and the peasant Confederation of Indigenous Nationalities (CONAI) ousted President Mahuad and tenuously 'ruled' Ecuador for nearly a week. International disapproval was strong. Finally, elected Vice-President Noboa took office, reinstating all of Mahuad's policies, including the full dollarisation of the Ecuadorian currency. Some of the colonels will be brought to trial and the CONAI militants threaten another coup if things don't change. While this seems like an empty threat now, it remains a stunning indictment of neo-liberal, IMF imposed policies that the first coup even happened at all.

## Dollars instead of sucres?

The newest measure taken by the government of President Gustavo Noboa, in an effort to pull Ecuador out of its current economic crisis, was the approval of the legal framework for the dollar plan. The package of 85 articles and 31 complementary clauses passed by Congress on March 1, by a vote of 63 to 60, would make the dollar the country's principal currency. Ecuador's Central Bank, which has US$1.26 billion in reserves, will have 180 days to exchange its sucres and establish mechanisms for carrying out all financial transactions in dollars.

While Assistant US Treasury Secretary for International Affairs Edwin Truman said his country has 'every intention to support this plan through international financial organisations,' opinion polls show that 74% of Ecuadorians oppose the dollar plan, fearing it would increase poverty. 'Many people are trying to create fear, doubt and uncertainty about this new plan, but what Ecuadorians should fear is the past, because that's what impoverished them,' Finance Minister Jorge Guzmán said.

## The dollarisation trap

(Saavedra, 1999)

One of the last decisions made by former Ecuadorian President Jamil Mahuad (1998-2000), who was forced out of office in January after an indigenous uprising, was to adopt the US dollar as the country's currency, a plan known in Ecuador as dollarisation, with the exchange rate set at 25,000 sucres to the dollar.

Interview with economist Alberto Acosta
*Why did Mahuad decide on the dollar plan?*
For political reasons, because Mahuad saw in the dollar plan a kind of life saver to prevent his fall, and in fact it did allow him to survive a little more than 10 days when he literally was already out the door. There are also economic reasons, not only President Mahuad's, but also those of the dominant classes who, by dollarising the Ecuadorian economy, publicly acknowledged their inability to maintain their own economic policy.
*How will this speed up the neo-liberal process in Ecuador?*
Because it represents defeat or inability on the part of the elites, it becomes a trap for ordinary Ecuadorians, because through the supposed magic solution of the dollar plan, they are trying to entrench the neo-liberal model, deepen its adjustments, move ahead with the privatisation of the petroleum industry, electricity, telephones, social security, and clear the way for flexibilisation of labour that will make work more precarious and weaken social forces. In addition, it will increase the Ecuadorian economy's dependence on trade with the US We will become a new North American market, annexed at no cost to them.
*What is Ecuador's position now in Latin America?*
We are marginalised again. We're turning our back on the process of horizontal integration. Instead of forming a Latin American bloc to negotiate better conditions with the US, by renouncing our currency we have renounced any equitable and symmetrical negotiation. At one point, we believed that when the moratorium was declared on payment of the

121

external debt (in September 1999) of Brady bonds and, later, Eurobonds, that could open up a new stage of re-negotiation of the external debt in Latin America. Nothing like that is going to happen. Because of the dollar plan, Ecuador will continue to be the least important player in this process.

*Who stands to benefit?*

Once we overcome the present stage of depression, the main beneficiaries will be importers. You can also see certain people promoting measures that supposedly favour production when they are really not producers but contraband dealers. The private international banking system will benefit, as will those companies that control services in general and privatised public services in particular. Stock markets will benefit if the economy improves and there is greater investment in variable-rate, rather than fixed-rate, instruments. In general, large merchants who can stand to sell their products over the long term will benefit.

*And who loses?*

The big loser is the country and its future. In the first ranks of losers are those who can't continue to work and who cannot recover with a new productive effort: pensioners. Big losers will also include people who will increasingly have to compete in a smaller market, such as taxi drivers and transport workers in general, and the productive apparatus in both agriculture and industry, which will take a beating from imports. The hope is that the dollar plan will attract foreign investment.

*Is this realistic?*

The simple fact of having an economy that operates in dollars isn't going to make us more productive, less corrupt, more competent or less inefficient. What will happen is a process that will return the Ecuadorian economy to a system of national production based more and more on raw materials — petroleum, agricultural products, forestry products, especially exploitation of wood, mining and some tourism. This is going to bring foreign investment based on the interests of transnational companies. I don't believe there will be a big turnaround or a great injection of fresh capital. In the first place, those who come will be bargain-hunters taking advantage of the big sale that will take place with the dollar plan, privatisation and flexibilisation of labour. There will be a de-nationalising of the economy.

*Where will the dollars come from to sustain the economy?*

Without dollars, there won't be an economy, there won't be production or consumption, there won't be money for investment or decentralisation, there won't be education or health care, there won't be a country. Therefore, we need dollars, and we'll get them by exporting, and that means having a policy of cheap labour — labour that is poorly paid, overworked, hired by the hour at less than 65 cents an hour, with no union or labour rights, and having to assume all costs, even those of social security, within those 65 cents.

*How will the dollar plan affect the environment?*

Ecuador's environment and the entire country will lose with greenbacks. We will produce more raw material. If we're talking now about a second oil pipeline, we're soon going to need a third pipeline to keep pumping out more and more petroleum, without worrying about the effects on nature and without immediately seeing its value reflected in the dollars that are going to be indispensable if we don't want to die of hunger.

*Is this process irreversible?*

No, definitely not. Even with a dollar plan, there will always be the possibility of going back if the country maintains its dignity and sovereignty, and works to see that its historic destiny is respected.

## Cochabamba takes on globalisation

On a smaller, local scale, and failing to garner the same international press coverage as the Ecuador coup, in February and April 2000, civil society organised and took to the streets in Cochabamba, in central Bolivia, against the government's privatisation of the department's water supply to a US and British consortium which had announced a 300% rate increase. For days battle raged. Veterans of social struggles claim it was the nastiest confrontation anywhere in the country in the last 50 years, and this not over a military dictatorship but over the foreign privatisation of a basic right – water. In the April confrontation the entire country came out in support of Cochabamba and to express their own local economic discontents. Some police in La Paz even mutineed for pay raises. The national

**Caribbean nations sell citizenship for dollars**
Some Caribbean island nations have discovered a new source of international finance in our globalised world – selling citizenship. For around US$50,000 you can get a new passport, even under a false name. The government of Dominica announced its foray into this business as a 'passport to paradise'. Critics, especially in Washington, however, see these practices as a way for criminals, especially from Russia and US tax evaders, to get around the law. Caribbean governments reply that this is a way to attract foreign capital at a time when their fragile economies are threatened by globalisation. Others see it as selling sovereignty cheap.

elected government of ex-dictator Hugo Banzer declared a 90 day state of siege throughout the country but the foreign water consortium was finally turned out. The state of siege was lifted early to facilitate the government's National Dialogue on poverty reduction, as required under HIPC II.

In the late 1980s, author of *A Fate Worse Than Debt*, Susan George, coined the phrase 'financial low intensity warfare' (FLIC) carried out by the North against the South and which doesn't seek absolute victory (total debt repayment) but rather long-term control and power by dealing with the problem with a divide and conquer strategy which allows leverage. 'The debt crisis is warfare in the most literal sense. The effect of debt on people's lives are almost exactly the same ones that one would see in the case of conventional warfare. [But] with debt the destruction is more gradual, it bleeds its victims but it never quite empties them' (Potter, 1998). More recently, in January 2000 in Lima, Peru, a friend of mine, economist Hugo Cabieses, taught me the phrase 'low intensity democracy' to describe what we are observing politically around the region in the new millennium. So it is.

# Chapter 8
# Alternative solutions?

The flurry of proposed millennium 'solutions' to the debt/financial/trade crises has already been alluded to in previous chapters. There is no doubt that the global Jubilee 2000 movement, and other civil society involvement, has had a tremendous, if not determinant, impact. Articles were written, books were published, meetings were convened, panels discussed the 'problems,' rock stars such as Bono from U2 and the Pope himself made pronouncements on what seemed to be a daily basis.

## Creditor responses

To date, many of the initiatives for resolving the crises have come from the North, and as such reflect the ideological bias of those governments and financial institutions. Indeed, for the creditor commercial banks, international financial institutions, Northern governments and their countries' elites, from the US to Asia, 'recovery' has largely been assured for the time being. Granted, the WTO is in a shambles, but this writer predicts its survival. The IMF got to sell part of its gold reserves while keeping them in stock, not unlike eating your cake and having it too. The World Bank is applauded for its renewed poverty focus, even as it and the IMF continued to exact draconian structural adjustment conditionalities from even the poorest Southern debtors with HIPC II. Eastern Europe may be a bit iffy, but Russia has become part of the G-7, making it the G-8. And, Northern governments are writing-off their moribund Southern bilateral debts in droves, but at the same time reducing their development assistance.

So is there a crisis after all? Yes, but for the poor and working classes in the South (and parts of the North). So a myriad of proposed 'solutions' proliferate, in large measure designed to protect and perpetuate the current global financial system rather than the vast majority of the world's population. Despite this proliferation of proposals, however, it is striking how similar many of them are. One cannot help but wonder what would happen if as much energy and commitment went into implementing *just* solutions as now go into designing *viable* proposals. Meanwhile, the poor are waiting with their dying breaths.

## Debtor countries' responses

There are many differences within the sovereign debtor community. Indeed, there are few things that tie so many different countries and cultures together except the fact that they borrowed money from Northern creditors and now are increasingly bound to a global trade and capital flows system, over which they have little control. In the past, Northern creditors used divide and conquer tactics (offering Mexico or Brazil lower interest rates and extended payback timeframes) to keep Southern debtor countries from forming any kind of 'cartel'. There now seems to be little threat of that happening.

Nonetheless, the mid-1997 Latin American Parliamentary Meeting on External Debt and the End of the Millennium, held in Caracas, Venezuela, did conclude with the following observations and recommendations. There was full recognition that what binds the Southern countries together is that they must 'obey' Northern imposed privatisation of their national sovereign assets, which enhances private global capital control over Southern governments, with little risk to the investors and scant return to the countries involved. As a result:

• public debt is the most powerful international mechanism to encourage international financial capital flows, which provide no real support, indeed hurt, debtor economies,

• this in turn severely impinges on national sovereignty,

• such capital flows and international 'investments' are often illegal under current Southern national constitutions,

• the people, especially the poor, are the ones who 'pay' and suffer most because of the recession caused,

• therefore, a Latin American debtors' union (cartel) is needed to protect Southern interests.

Recommendations to address these realities included:

• take legally abusive cases to the World Court
• support the global Jubilee 2000 movement
• enlist the African Parliamentary group to join forces
• promote information campaigns
• protect the environment
• re-evaluate real remaining debt levels and fair interest rates
• current and future negotiations with Northern creditors should not be seen as justifying past debts.

In reviewing these observations and recommendations, two things stand out. One, that while the analysis is far-reaching, the recommendations are geared to reform. Secondly, this gathering was of parliamentarians, not heads of state and their finance ministers. During the two Latin American Summits in the second half of the 1990s (Miami and Santiago), the discourse hovered much more closely on promoting of trade and international financial flows, rather than curtailing them.

African governments' heads of state have been much more outspoken in the 1990s in calling for true structural changes. In January 2000 African leaders met to discuss the economic agenda for the continent in the new millennium and requested that no new conditionalities be imposed upon them from the World Bank and IMF, insisting that the PRSP should not be used to impose a political mandate for poverty reduction but should be a means for organising how it is accomplished.

## NGO responses

Labour, environmental, development, church, women's and other coalitions of NGOs have been outspoken proponents for debt relief, a new development model and re-organisation of the global economic system for nearly two decades. Below is a summary of proposals in the new millennium. However, even the most benevolent and well-meaning reformist proposals are unlikely to bring about enough change to bring about an equitable future, since they are cast within the parameters of the current world economic order.

There is no dispute that the global Jubilee 2000 movement is the world leader in calling for equitable change and reform. Some pundits believe it to be the largest civil society effort in history. While environmentalists, feminists and others might disagree, nonetheless, what the movement has achieved is truly impressive and commendable.

'The Jubilee 2000 Coalition is advocating a debt-free start to the Millennium for a billion people through the one-off cancellation of the unpayable debts of the world's poorest countries by the year 2000, under a fair and transparent process. Creditors as well as debtors must accept responsibility for these high levels of indebtedness. The campaign is based on the scriptural idea of the Jubilee Year. Every 7x7 years (i.e. every 49 years), debts are forgiven and slaves set free. The campaign was launched in 1996 by three major Christian agencies in Britain and by the World Development Movement. In October 1977 a coalition was formed [and] now comprises over 70 members. Jubilee 2000 is also being promoted in over 50 countries around the world.'

## Jubilee 2000

From the Jubilee 2000/USA come the following proposals:

- Impoverished people should not bear the burden of debt,
- The burden of debt should be shared equally by debtor and creditor governments, institutions and individuals who were involved in making or benefiting from the original loan agreements,
- External factors beyond the control of debtors should be addressed by those who have the power to alleviate them,
- Developing nations should not be forced to sacrifice their political self-determination or economic self-reliance in order to receive debt relief,
- Long-term solutions should promote just international economic relationships that will prevent future crises.

Southern Jubilee 2000 campaigns, notably those of Jubilee 2000-South, Jubilee 2000-Afrika, and Jubilee 2000 Latin America/Caribbean, have taken stronger positions than their Northern colleagues (see below). Even within national and regional efforts there has been discord. For example, Jubilee 2000/USA supported and lobbied for US Congressional approval of HIPC I and II and IMF gold sales, while others, like the 50 Years is Enough campaign, did not, pointing out that the former have onerous structural adjustment conditionalities and the latter simply shores up the IMF. Jubilee South rejected the Cologne G-7/8 accords as a 'cruel hoax' which keeps the South 'in the game' but only deals with 2% of Southern debt and no real poverty issues. These internal NGO disputes have at times been close to 'bloody,' to quote several insiders, but more disruptive has been the IFIs' and national governments' ability to use these disagreements to their advantage, either coopting some of the more reformist NGOs into their ranks or claiming that such civil society discourse clearly shows that there is no consistent voice for the poor and disenfranchised.

> **Jubilee is not enough**
>
> Jubilee 2000/USA released a statement after the September 1999 joint IMF/World Bank annual meetings pointing out that these institutions had not met the global Jubilee 2000 1998 Rome Declaration goals of rejecting conditionalities and an enhanced role for the IFIs; they also pointed out that the amount of debt relief being offered was 'too little, too late,' and called for debt relief to be additional to, not in lieu of ODA. Nonetheless, Jubilee 2000/USA successfully continued to lobby the US Congress for HIPC II funding and IMF gold sales.

## No to debt, yes to life – Jubilee 2000

(Excerpted from Jubilee 2000 Latin America/Caribbean Platform Declaration, 1999)

The foreign debt of the so-called Third World, by its exorbitant amount and rate of growth and ever worse conditionalities, precludes socio-economic development of four/fifths of the world's population.

Debt is a direct expression of the unjust global economic order which is the result of a long history of slavery, exploitation and terms of trade which are detrimental to the poor.

The external debt in Latin America during the mid-1970s was some US$60 billion; in 1980 it reached US$204 billion; in 1990 it was US$443 billion and it is calculated by 1999 to reach US$706 billion, requiring US$123 billion in debt service alone. The region paid US$739 billion in debt service from 1982-1996, more than its total accumulated debt.

Under these circumstances the external debt is unpayable, illegitimate and immoral.

The creditors' rescue operations, with the help of the World Bank and IMF, including HIPC, have only served to guarantee the mechanisms of debt slavery.

Jubilee 2000 Latin America/Caribbean demands:

Cancellation of the immoral and illegal Third World debt in 2000AD according to these principles:

- transparency and inclusiveness
- limits future debt service ratios to no more than 3% of the annual national budget
- creation of a representative Arbitration Tribunal. For example, Jubilee 2000/Brazil convened a People's Tribunal to judge the legitimacy of Brazil's foreign debt. After hearing testimony from debt experts and representatives of the Landless Peoples Movement, the unemployed, pensioners and trades unionists, the Tribunal concluded that much of Brazil's debt is unjust and illegitimate.
- Take into account the South's right to development in debt negotiations
- Undertake national debt audits throughout the region with ample civil society participation
- Assure that financial 'savings' of debt cancellation are spent on social and environmental programs, especially job creation, education, health and social security – with special emphasis on the most vulnerable groups such as children, women, the elderly and indigenous – and guarantee the active participation of civil society in the design, execution and evaluation of these processes

129

- Transform the current economic and financial world system such that it serves people and is based on just international relations, equity and solidarity among countries and people – in this context it is necessary to strengthen the UN system, restoring its original functions now usurped by other institutions
- Total rejection of the Multilateral Investment Agreement for the absolute subordination it implies for men, women, people and countries confronting the (il)logic of the free market and capital.

We call on (Jubilee 2000) campaigns in the North to support our demands and especially ask these Jubilee 2000 Northern campaigns to never propose resolutions or laws regarding the debt which are less than we demand.

The fact that the Jubilee 2000 movement in Latin America/Caribbean, and in general in the South, feel the need to put out such strong statements reflects the differences they see between their demands and those of Jubilee 2000 in the North. The changes called for in the South are more fundamental and structural to the management of the whole economy, and not only concerned with reform of debt negotiation. As can be seen below, the differences are more than rhetorical.

## We are not debtors, we are owed!

### External Debt/The South-South Summit in South Africa

(Edited from Briceño, 2000)

The logic of the struggle is reversed. Since the J2K South-South Summit, the campaign against further debt payments and in favour of cancelling the South's debts has refined its position. The People of the South not only demand the repudiation and cancellation of their debts to the North but now, are taking the offensive, reclaiming their rights as creditors of ecological, social and historical debts for the harm caused by the industrialised countries of the North. This new vision of the problem proposed that the North pay reparations to the South and converts the J2K-South campaign into a movement of movements with commons concerns and agenda.

Is the debt the cause of oppression or the consequence of an economic system that strangles the weakest? Debt is a problem of life or death for the people of the South. It is an instrument of exploitation and control of Third World countries and is used to open these economies to the globalised neo-liberal system. For this reason, we propose the definitive closing of the World Bank, the IMF and the WTO and that the fight to cancel the debt become primarily a fight for a new society, inspired by relations of solidarity, focused on human needs and not on capital.

The South's debt to the North has already been paid through debt service payments and SAPs. These debts were not only illegitimate but they were also paid. Now the South demands that the North pay for reparations of harm caused for decades and centuries of oppression and colonisation. The South also demands that the North pay its ecological debt. The ransacking of natural resources and genocide of millions of people needs to be repaid. Who owes who?

Another conclusion of the Summit was that the notion of North/South is much more than geographical. The North is characterised by being the centre of power, imperialism, which also has its allies and agents in the South who defend their interests; it is also the IFIs which industrialised countries use also to defend their privilege. The South is the periphery – workers, unemployed, those excluded from society – even if they live in the North geographically, for they are also victims of neo-liberal policies – it is the people of the North and South who must make common cause to change the economic system that has made a religion out of the dictatorships of capital and trade.

Debt relief is a tactic to divide and conquer us. Debt relief and poverty reduction programs are a subterfuge of the creditor countries and IFIs. Their objective is to recycle unpayable debts in order to maintain the alleged legitimacy of those debts and therefore assure the debtor countries remain in the debt service game. To only deal with the poorest and most indebted countries (HIPC) is a perverse tactic of the creditors to divide the debtors once more and weaken our resolve for a just debt cancellation. This creditors' offensive enlists the IFIs to manipulate and coopt NGOs and put them at the service of neo-liberal interests with rhetoric of civil society participation.

### For a debt-free millennium

(Excerpted from the Buenos Aires Jubilee 2000 Latin America & Caribbean Coalition Declaration)

'…We maintain our conviction that the foreign debt is immoral and illegitimate, reasons for which our people should not be forced to repay it. Not only did they not benefit from the debt but they also did not participate in its accrual. In this respect, even though we celebrate the mobilisation that has been able to place this problem on the world public agenda, we do not accept the Cologne Debt Initiative announced by the G-7/8 as a step toward the resolution of the problem. We reject its insistence on maintaining HIPC conditionality and Structural Adjustment as prerequisites for debt cancellation. We also reject the increased meddling of the IMF in the design and control of policies that affect our lives…

131

Resolving the foreign debt problem entails seeking historic reparations that the countries of the North owe to the people of the South as a consequence of the looting and devastation that they have carried out over 500 years and currently continue through the implementation of Structural Adjustment Programs, the conditioning of new investments, free trade agreements, and other policies which increase the Social and Ecological Debt which are due to our people and seriously affect their human rights and democratic freedoms.

(We commit to) strengthen strategies of mobilisation and education of our people as means for deepening consciousness and building a culture of solidarity that will enable those sectors now excluded to fully exercise their rights.

(We will) include and highlight experiences of popular resistance, legal battles and the formation of ethical tribunals against foreign debt, both nationally and internationally, so as to promote and strengthen our demands and proposals.

(We will) integrate visions which include a gender/justice perspective that favours the building of new, more democratic, just and egalitarian social relations.

In the face of the mechanisms of domination established through the system of neo-liberal globalisation, we subscribe to and propose the globalisation of South/South and South/North solidarity, by joining together with other movements and social change agents nationally, regionally and globally.'

## Which way for NGOs?

(Bendaña, 1999)

The increasing prominence of non-governmental organisations (NGOs) is, on balance, one of the few welcome developments in contemporary post-cold war politics. However, from the standpoint of someone who has worked with both governments and NGOs in the South, their increasing influence raises some concerns and merits more discussion among analysts and activists.

Today, few governmental or intergovernmental bodies dispute the notion that 'civil society' and NGOs deserve a hearing in the determination of important policies and decisions. In their country visits, World Bank and even the IMF missions now often make the rounds with non-governmental entities, including labour unions and opposition parties. Within multilateral institutions, new bureaucratic offices are created to deal with governance, civil society, and NGOs. Sometimes these visiting officials even take note of what NGO members have to say, although they mostly feign interest, not being quite sure how to interpret what has been said.

NGOs are growing in influence – or at least in voice – particularly in the North. And there are few issues that do not relate to the expertise and concern of one civic organisation or another. So prevalent and engaged are NGOs that Northern governments increasingly feel obliged (or find it convenient) to provide funding and contracts. NGOs have forged new relationships with governments on issues from democratic governance to the environment, women's concerns to election monitoring, landmine eradication to appropriate technology and food security.

But is it not a problem that NGOs appear to be gaining terrain at the expense of political parties and democratic social movements? Does NGOisation entail de-politisation along with defensive retreats into localism or globalism at the expense of national transformation? In fact, NGO influence appears to be displacing traditional politics, including traditional labour union activities. Traditional political ways of exercising citizenship and collective struggle appear to be giving way to a more conservative and much-touted rise of 'civil society.'

There is an international dimension as the 'new' politics of civil society and NGOs – spawned by the North – descend as the latest wave of the white man's burden on the South. Swelling in the aftermath of the cold war, the NGO sector continues to expand and is spreading to the South. Many of the Northern-based forms of NGO and civil society organisation are being uncritically exported to and imported by the South with mixed and as yet inconclusive results.

For the South, this proliferation of NGOs – both local and Northern – may pose more long-range problems than opportunities, especially when considering the many structural obstacles to social change in the South. But this should not be exclusively a concern of Southern progressives. If global change is imperative to global survival, and if the rise of international NGOs is part of the change, then the problems associated with the ambiguous role of NGOs operating in the South should be a concern for us all.

Whether we choose to admit it or not, NGOs take part in a global contest that may be won or lost on the basis of ideology and consciousness. Throughout history, capitalism's principal weapon has been in the realm of culture and ideology. In many ways, development and advocacy NGOs reflect the crisis of the left, which is mostly a crisis of intellectuals involving an outright failure of nerve that is unfortunately being transmitted to the South and communities in struggle. Some of us would like to know, for example, if advocates believe that the basic Marxist critique of capitalism is valid, and if not, what do they offer as an alternative analytical framework. Are we now all called upon to follow the lead of ex-leftists in the North in discovering 'civil society' and 'NGO engagement?' Do we then go on to embrace identity politics and cultural relativism to fill in the gaps left by global neoliberalism?

On the other hand, the 'traditional' left, North and South, must relate to changing expressions of politics, including NGOs. Labour unions, for example, that ignored the growing *maquila* industry in Central America found their place quickly supplanted by women's associations and their NGO supporters abroad. Some parties and unions in Latin America are reaching out constructively to the unprecedented spread of activity and civic organisation among women, youth, human rights activists, ecologists, communal and ethnic movements, and sometimes even gay ones, although this is more difficult for the 'machistas-leninistas.' Other parties are slower, and some insist that the organised working class still has its traditional leading role to play in social advancement.

NGOs and advocacy campaigns will have an important role to play in global issues demanding global responses. They can be good advocates and channel funds to local development efforts. But let us not underestimate the power of the global power structure, which is reflected in its capacity to absorb the pressures of superficial change as a defence against deeper challenges. Like social and patriarchal systems, the global apparatus will allow some change to take place and in the process leave the deep structures untouched and even invisible.

Part of the problem, from our perspective, is that many national and international NGOs are derisive about politics at the national level – sometimes with good reason. But our organisations should not follow the path of ex-left academics who claim to be making a virtue of necessity by joining the chorus condemning state intervention and the struggle for state power. There is a danger in 'small is beautiful.' Given interlocking national and international power structures, the sum of 'local' democracies does not equal national or international democracy. However, until some other system is invented, local elections and political parties do make a difference. Perhaps not everyone is ready to turn their backs on the need to attain representation at the national level, because, at this stage at least, the democracy movement cannot afford to dispense with the nation-state.

Finally, all of us, as NGOs, should constantly remind ourselves that the principal efforts and sacrifices to attain development, democracy, and peace with justice will be made, as always, by the impoverished. It follows that they, a majority in the South, should be the principal beneficiaries, lest we continue to be confused by the amorphous notion of civil society. NGOs have done very positive work – particularly when they've worked with and not simply for people. But we must also envision a steady and systematic replacement of NGOs with people's organisations capable of acting at the local, national, and international levels. The internationalisation and concentration of capital and power must be followed by the internationalisation of people's movements and organisations. Therein lies our task.

## Northern responses

In addition to Jubilee 2000-specific proposals there are other Northern NGO propositions that merit review, though it should be borne in mind that most of them come from individual Jubilee 2000 member organisations. The following are presented in alphabetical order, not of importance:

• Bretton Woods Institutions – 'In as much as the IMF and World Bank have failed to oversee the international financial system in a manner that supports sustainable and productive development, they should either be fundamentally restructured or new institutions put in their place' (*Alternatives for the Americas*)

• Capital controls – 'Since the Asian crisis, these have gained some new legitimacy in official circles but would not be allowed under NAFTA or probably a new FTAA.' Nonetheless, measures (like those used in Chile), which require foreign investors to deposit a portion of the capital they bring into a country in an interest free account with the central bank or require foreign portfolio investment to remain within a country for a minimum period would be useful. The Rio de Janeiro Declaration issued by the Civil Society Forum for Dialogue Europe-Latin America/Caribbean (June 1999) calls for a reversal of financial liberalisation and the implementation of controls over international capital flows through taxation on international investments. (see Tobin Tax below).

• Conditionality alternatives – These could include social benchmarks such as poverty or human development indicators developed through a transparent and civil society participatory process.

• Debt standstill and work-out procedure – The guidelines laid out by the G-7/8 finance ministers are a step forward in involving the private sector as responsible for bearing the consequences of their risk investments and recognising that taxpayers in both the North (via the IFIs) and the South (via socialisation of private sector bank rescues) should not bear the total cost. However, as one investor cynically observed, 'asking the lenders to help save the debtor countries is like asking the iceberg to save the Titanic.' UNCTAD has already done work on this and should work with the UN, G-7/8 and IMF to develop a new mechanism administered by a new body such as an International Debt Tribunal.

- Foreign investment – No international investment treaty, such as the FTAA, or institution such as the WTO, should prevent governments from enforcing performance requirements that serve economic development, environmental or other legitimate objectives. Governments should have the right to encourage productive investments that increase links between the local and national economy (as well as the world economy) and limit investments that make no net contribution to development, especially speculative investments that lead to volatility, rapid capital outflows and economic crises.

- Structural Adjustment Participatory Review International Network (SAPRI – headed by the Development Group for Alternative Policies – D-GAP – in Washington, DC) – This was originally organised around a major initiative taken with World Bank President James Wolfensohn to assess in 10 countries, through civil society/government/Bank collaboration, the impact of various adjustment measures on a range of population groups and socio-economic sectors. SAPRI is designed to yield recommendations to the World Bank and governments for changes in economic adjustment programmes and in economic-policymaking processes. SAPRI is also legitimising an active role for civil society in economic decision-making and, if successful, will give governments greater flexibility to respond to the needs and priorities of their own people rather than to the dictates of international creditors.

- Tobin Tax – The introduction of an international tax on currency transactions which currently globally amount to US$1.5 *trillion* a day. The tax would reduce the  opportunity for certain kinds of speculation based on making a profit on small anomalies in currency exchange rates. Because the differences are so small, even a minimal tax (say 0.25%) would raise the cost of such currency trade above the expected gain. For long term investments the tax should not be onerous because it would be small compared to the expected gains. The intention of the tax is to discourage speculative flows of international capital.

Even if these and other far reaching and well intentioned propositions were successful in achieving the smoother functioning of global capital markets and debt reduction, they would not be adequate to ensure better global outcomes in terms of growth, equity and stability. These proposals are still largely founded on continuing and reforming the current system.

In a survey of the proposals currently on offer, *The Economist* wearily observed that, 'Financial crises occur with monotonous regularity, and are followed just as regularly by demands for a new (financial) architecture.' Its analysis concluded that the current financial problems are simply not severe enough, at least in the G-7 countries, to overcome large political obstacles to radical change. Something as seismic as the Bretton Woods Conference, which gave birth to the IMF (and World Bank), came only after a world war and the Great Depression had forced policy makers into sweeping reforms. (Green, 1999).

## The Non-governmental order: will NGOs democratise, or merely disrupt, global governance?

(*The Economist*, 11-17 December 1999)

As politicians pore over the disarray in Seattle, they might look to citizens' groups for advice. The non-governmental organisations (NGOs) that descended on Seattle were a model of everything the trade negotiators were not. They were well organised. They built unusual coalitions (environmentalists and labour groups, for instance, bridged old gulfs to jeer the WTO together). They had a clear agenda – to derail the talks. And they were masterly users of the media.

The battle of Seattle is only the latest and most visible in a string of recent NGO victories. The watershed was the Earth Summit in Rio de Janeiro in 1992, when the NGOs roused enough public pressure to push through agreements on controlling greenhouse gases. In 1994, protesters dominated the World Bank's anniversary meeting with a *Fifty Years is Enough* campaign, and forced a rethink of the Bank's goals and methods. In 1998, an ad hoc coalition of consumer rights activists and environmentalists helped to sink the Multilateral Agreement on Investment (MAI), a draft treaty to harmonise rules on foreign investment under the aegis of the OECD. In the past couple of years another global coalition of NGOs, Jubilee 2000, has pushed successfully for a dramatic reduction in the debts of the poorest countries....

In short, citizens' groups are increasingly powerful at the corporate, national and international level. How they have become so, and what this means, are questions that urgently need to be addressed. Are citizens' groups, as many of their supporters claim, the first steps towards an 'international civil society' (whatever that might be)? Or do they represent a dangerous shift of power to unelected and unaccountable special-interest groups?

Over the past decade, NGOs and their memberships have grown hugely Although organisations like these have existed for generations and had a powerful part in abolishing slavery laws, the social and economic shifts of this decade have given them new life. The end of communism, the spread of democracy in poor countries, technological change and economic integration – globalisation, in short – have created fertile soil for the rise of NGOs. Globalisation itself has exacerbated a host of worries: over the environment, labour rights, human rights, consumer rights and so on. Democratisation

137

and technological progress have revolutionised the way in which citizens can unite to express their disquiet.

Citizens' groups play roles that go far beyond political activism. Many are important deliverers of services, especially in developing countries. As a group, NGOs now deliver more aid than the whole United Nations system. Some of the biggest NGOs are primarily aid providers. Others, such as Oxfam, are both aid providers and campaigners. Others still, such as (Jubilee 2000), stick to campaigning. And it is here that technological change is having its biggest impact.

When groups could communicate only by telephone, fax or mail, it was prohibitively expensive to share information or build links between different organisations. Now information can be dispersed quickly, and to great effect, online. The MAI was already in trouble when a draft of the text, posted on the Internet by an NGO, allowed hundreds of hostile watchdog groups to mobilise against it. Similarly, the Seattle trade summit was disrupted by dozens of web sites which alerted everyone (except, it seems, the Seattle police), to the protests that were planned.

New coalitions can be built online. Much of the pre-Seattle coalition building between environmental and citizens' groups, for instance, was done by e-mail. About 1,500 NGOs signed an anti-WTO protest declaration set up online by Public Citizen, a consumer-rights group. More important, the Internet allows new partnerships between groups in rich and poor countries. Armed with compromising evidence of local labour practices or environmental degradation from southern NGOs, for example, activists in developed countries can attack corporations much more effectively.

This phenomenon – amorphous groups of NGOs, linked online, descending on a target – has been dubbed an 'NGO swarm' in a RAND study. And such groups are awful for governments to deal with. An NGO swarm, say the RAND researchers, has no 'central leadership or command structure; it is multi-headed, impossible to decapitate'. And it can sting a victim to death.

Less dramatic, but just as important, is the rise of NGOs that are dubbed by Sylvia Ostry, a trade expert from the University of Toronto, as 'technical' groups. These specialise in providing highly sophisticated analysis and information, and they can be crucial to the working of some treaties. In the campaign to cut third-world debt, a handful of NGOs, have become as expert in the minutiae of debt-reduction procedures as the bureaucrats at the IMF and World Bank. Increasingly, they have been co-opted into making policy. At the WTO, these technical NGOs [...] have concentrated on training and providing information on the arcana of trade law to delegates from poor countries.

If the power of NGOs has increased in a globalised world, who has lost out? A popular view is that national governments have. In an article in Foreign Affairs in 1997, Jessica Mathews, the head of the Carnegie Endowment for International Peace, wrote that 'the steady concentration of power in the hands of states that began in 1648 with the Peace of Westphalia, is over, at least for a while.' Certainly national governments no longer have a monopoly of information, or an unequalled reach, compared to corporations and civil society. But the real losers in this power shift are international organisations.

Less obvious is whether NGO attacks will democratise, or merely disable, these organisations. At first sight, Seattle suggests a pessimistic conclusion: inter-governmental outfits will become paralysed in the face of concerted opposition. History, however, suggests a different outcome. Take the case of the World Bank. The Fifty Years is Enough campaign of 1994 was a prototype of Seattle (complete with activists invading the meeting halls). Now the NGOs are surprisingly quiet about the World Bank. The reason is that the Bank has made a huge effort to co-opt them.

James Wolfensohn, the Bank's boss, has made 'dialogue' with NGOs a central component of the institution's work. More than 70 NGO specialists work in the Bank's field offices. More than half of World Bank projects last year involved NGOs. Mr Wolfensohn has built alliances with everyone, from religious groups to environmentalists. His efforts have diluted the strength of 'mobilisation networks' and increased the relative power of technical NGOs (for it is mostly these that the Bank has co-opted). From environmental policy to debt relief, NGOs are at the centre of World Bank policy. Often they determine it. The new World Bank is more transparent, but it is also more beholden to a new set of special interests.

The WTO will not evolve in the same way. As a forum where governments set rules that bind rich as well as poor countries, it is inherently more controversial. Nor does it disburse money for projects, making it harder to co-opt NGOs. But it could still try to weaken the broad coalition that attacked it in Seattle by reaching out to mainstream and technical NGOs. Some will celebrate this as the advent of the age when huge institutions will heed the voice of Everyman. Others will complain that self-appointed advocates have gained too much influence. What is certain is that a new kind of actor is claiming, loudly, a seat at the table.

## Southern NGOs

(Excerpted from Bello, 1999)

One of Asia's (and the world's) leading NGO alternatives spokespersons is Walden Bello from the Thailand-based *Focus on the Global South*.

It is against this dismal background that we now move to the question of reform. Here one does not feel like taking the path of those who, after indicting the Bretton Woods Institutions, do a turnaround when asked for solutions and appeal to the BWIs and the WTO to become answerable to the UN and reorient their policies to serve the interests of the world's poor majority since this would be 'truly in the enlightened self-interest of people in the rich, industrialised countries, their children, and their children's children.' This is utopian thinking, especially at a time that the North has just completed a campaign of global rollback that has delivered the coup de grace of the Southern project of reform. For reform, not revolution, was what the New International Economic Order (NIEO), the Non-Aligned Movement, and UNCTAD was all about and look where this already very limited enterprise, what one Northern observer described as 'the present order, with extra helpings for the flag bearers of the South' got the Third World.

### Human Rights

'Human rights were born against power abuses. They still are a very effective tool against authoritarian regimes. The critique of human rights should not result in throwing the baby out with the bath water.'

Esteva and Prakash, 1998a

Change at this time means not spending or wasting time trying to enlarge areas of reform within the World Bank, IMF and WTO. They are, to borrow a phrase from Max Weber, an iron cage of three overlapping bureaucracies and mandates where Southern aspirations and interests are structurally constrained.

The project of making the UN agencies the pillars of an alternative global order is not going to result for a long, long time. What then should Southern movements for global reform focus their energies on? The main thrust, in our view, is to overload the system, to make it non-functional by constantly pushing demands that cannot be met by the system. The success of a strategy of overloading the system depends on creating global political alliances, including coalitions with anti-globalisation social and political forces in the North (the Seattle WTO debacle comes to mind).

Where structures are hopeless, the next best solution is to have non-functioning structures or no operative structures at all. It was, for instance, during a period where no bodies supervised aid and development – the Second World War era and immediate post-war era – that the countries of Latin America were able to successfully engage in import substitution to build up industrial structures. And it was during the period from the 1960s up to the late 1980s, before the establishment of the WTO, that the NICs of East and Southeast Asia were able to marry domestic protectionism to mercantilism to move from underdevelopment to industrial status in one generation.

Although the threat of unilateral action by the powerful is ever present, on balance a global system where there are either no or ineffective multilateral structures works to the benefit of the South. For the principal objective of most multilateral or international arrangements in history has never been to assure law and order to protect the weak. These structures have been pushed by the strong mainly to reduce the tremendous cost of policing the system to ensure that the less powerful do not cease to respect the rules set by the more powerful or break away completely.

In short, a fluid international system, where there are multiple zones of ambiguity that the less powerful can exploit in order to protect their interests, may be the only realistic alternative to the current global multilateral order that would weaken the hold of the North. The fewer structures and the less clear the rules, the better for the South.

## Alternative agendas

A significant change in the 1990s is that many African and Asian NGOs are now noticeably more 'radical' than their Latin American/Caribbean counterparts, who earlier were considered the vanguard. Whether this is a 'natural' historical evolutionary process or a potentially more sinister cooptation process within the 'more mature' Western NGO movement is a fascinating question for another book.

It is interesting to note in these regards that the UN General Assembly has called for a 'high level' meeting including the World Bank, IMF, WTO, UN, to deal with international financing, debt and development. South African President Thabo Mbeki has also convened a South/South alternative to the G-7/8 to present a united front at international fora. South Africa, China, India, Brazil, the Philippines, Argentina, Malaysia and Nigeria are to lead the way with other Southern nations invited in a body called G-77.

141

## More fundamental and viable civil society alternatives?

Throughout the research and writing of this book, I assiduously sought references to more 'radical' social movements current in the region today. The only one that stands out is the Zapatista and related initiatives in the poorest areas of Mexico.

The dawn of 1 January 1994 heralded the birth of NAFTA and the public emergence of the Mexican National Zapatista Liberation Army (EZLN). 'The ideological slant of the EZLN's declarations was puzzling: a guerrilla movement struggling for democracy, without aspirations to power or a (clear) leftist orientation? An Indian movement not showing ethnic fundamentalism but opposing NAFTA? A movement of illiterate peasants talking about transnational capital and using electronic networks to gain support for their struggle? The EZLN launched an eloquent and unprecedented attack upon the process of 'development.' Rather than demanding the expansion of the economy, either state or market-led, the EZLN sought to expel it from their domain. Is this the last episode of the era of the Central American guerrillas, or a local uprising that will soon vanish? Is this another outmoded and doomed Leninist attempt to organise the peasantry, join the party and smash the state? Or is it the first revolution of the 21$^{st}$ century, which may have profound effects in Mexico and elsewhere, and teach many lessons about contemporary, post-modern forms of social struggle and political power? [ ] The EZLN dares to declare to the world that development has failed miserably,' (Esteva,1999).

I don't know if the Zapatista experience is as hopeful and transferable as its proponents suggest. But at the cusp of the millennia nothing else presents itself more convincingly.

By simply eliminating the debt or curtailing financial flows the problems of the South will not be solved if the dominant, Northern-imposed, neo-liberal, export-led growth development paradigm remains. Indeed, as one crisis replaces another, the greatest danger may well be that just enough reform and relief will be provided to sustain the current system without fundamentally changing it. What the South most needs now is a measurable degree of self-reliance adequate to ensure current and future equitable relations with the North. Ultimately, it is the vast majority of people in the South who should determine their own production, distribution and consumption, not foreigners and national elites with a vested interest in maintaining the poor's dependency.

The popular cry of the people in the South should inform the solutions

Economically, *the debt has been paid*
Ethically, *no more should be paid*
Politically, *no more will be paid*

# Acronyms

| | |
|---|---|
| AID (also known as USAID) | US Agency for International Development |
| AOA | Agreement on Agriculture (WTO) |
| ALADI | Latin American Association for Integration |
| APEC | Asia Pacific Economic Cooperation |
| BWIs | Bretton Woods Institutions |
| CAL | capital account liberalization |
| CAP | Common Agricultural Policy (EU) |
| CARICOM | Caribbean Common Market |
| CDF | Comprehensive Development Framework |
| CEPAL | Economic Commission for Latin America and the Caribbean (UN) |
| ECLAC | Economic Commission of Latin America and the Caribbean |
| ESAF | enhanced structural adjustment facility |
| ESF | emergency social fund (usually World Bank) |
| EU | European Union |
| EZLN | Zapatista Army of National Liberation |
| FDI | foreign direct investment |
| FTAA | Free Trade Area of the Americas |
| FY | Financial Year |
| G7/8 | Group of 7 world's most industrialised countries (with Russia – 8) |
| GATT | General Agreement on Tariffs and Trade |
| GDP | gross domestic product |
| GNP | gross national product |
| HIPC | highly indebted poor country |
| IBRD | International Bank for Reconstruction and Development (World Bank) |
| IDA | International Development Association (World Bank) |
| IDB | Inter-American Development Bank |
| IFC | International Financial Corporation (World Bank) |
| IFIs | international financial institution(s) |
| IMF | International Monetary Fund |
| ITO | International Trade Organisation |

| | |
|---|---|
| LDC | less (or least) developed country |
| MERCOSUR | Southern Cone Common Market (Brazil, Argentina, Paraguay, Uruguay) |
| MIGA | Multilateral Investment Guarantee Agency (World Bank) |
| MDB | multilateral development bank (World Bank and the regional banks) |
| MNC | multinational corporation |
| NAFTA | North American Free Trade Agreement |
| NGO | non-governmental organisation |
| NIC | newly industrialised country |
| ODA | overseas development assistance (aid) |
| OECD | Organisation for Economic Co-operation and Development |
| OPEC | Oil Producing Export Countries |
| SAF | structural adjustment facility |
| SAL | structural adjustment loan |
| SAP | structural adjustment programme |
| SEAL | sectoral adjustment loan |
| TNC | transnational corporation |
| TRIMS | trade related investment measures (WTO) |
| TRIPS | trade related intellectual property rights (WTO) |
| UNCTAD | UN Conference on Trade and Development |
| US | United States |
| WTO | World Trade Organisation |

# Glossary

Balance of payments – a country's receipts and expenditures in international trade and financial transactions.

Billion – 1. one thousand million, 2. (formerly, in Britain) a million million (see trillion).

Bretton Woods System/Institutions (BWI) – usually refers to the International Monetary Fund (IMF) and World Bank (IBRD).

Capital account – the part of the balance of payments which details capital flows other than grants in and out of the country.

Capital account liberalisation (CAL) – the removal of restrictions on foreign-exchange transactions relating to capital flows; the term is increasingly used as shorthand for the proposal to extend the mandate of the IMF to include liberalisation of financial transfers.

Civil society – organisations such as churches, trade unions, NGOs and women's and environmental groups that are neither part of government nor the private for profit sector (though the latter may be included)

Commercial debt – owed to private creditors like banks or suppliers.

Concessional loans – loans provided with very favourable interest rates and repayment schedules, usually for development projects.

Conditionality – World Bank and IMF conditions attached to the loans provided.

Contagion/contamination – the phenomenon whereby developments in one country's economy lead to similar development in other countries.

Contingent Credit Line – a new form of IMF loan introduced in Spring 1999; intended to prevent contagion -no country had applied for this kind of loan by the end of 1999.

Current account – part of the balance of payments which details the difference between receipts for exports of goods and services and expenditure on imports of goods and services , plus grants from official creditors and workers' remittances.

Debt conversion – a way for creditors to get rid of some loans by converting them to securities that can be sold to third parties, thus reducing the creditor's risk.

Debt forgiveness – when a creditor cancels a debtor's obligation to repay a loan.

Debt overhang – the excess of a country's external debt over its long-term capacity to pay, which discourages adjustment, investment and development.

Debt repudiation (also known as 'default') – the refusal to recognise a debt obligation.

Debt service payments- payment made by a country on the amount of money owed to all its creditors each year for the interest and principal of its debt.

Debt service ratio – the ratio of debt service payments to the value of a country's exports.

Debt standstill – temporary cessation of debt repayments, giving a country a breathing space in which to renegotiate its debt obligations.

Debt swaps – when a creditor sells part of a debtor's outstanding loans at a discount to third parties.

Emerging markets – Southern economies that have become of interest to Northern investors in recent years thanks to a mixture of industrial development and policy measures such as capital account liberalisation and privatisation.

Enhanced Structural Adjustment Facility (ESAF) – IMF facility established in 1987 to provide concessional loans, conditioned on the implementation of certain economic policies, to low-income member countries facing long-term balance of payment problems (replaced in 1999 by PRSP).

Eurodollars – claims to US dollars held by banks, businesses and individuals outside the US.

External debt – public and private debt that is owed outside a country

Foreign direct investment (FDI) – investment abroad, usually by transnational corporations.

G-7/8 (Group of 7, now 8) – wealthy industrialised nations including the US, UK, Germany, France, Japan, Italy, Canada and now Russia.

GATT (General Agreement on Tariffs and Trade) – from 1946 until 1995, the major global forum for negotiations aimed at reducing tariffs and other barriers to free trade as controlled by the industrialised Northern countries.

Globalisation (economic) – the integration of local and national markets into the international market.

Gross Domestic Product (GDP) – the annual value of all goods and services produced within a country.

Gross National Product (GNP) – GDP plus the income residents receive from abroad for labour and capital, less similar payments to non-residents who contribute to the domestic economy.

Herd instinct – the tendency for investors to follow each other when making the decision whether or not to invest or disinvest in/from a country or sector.

International Bank for Reconstruction and Development (IBRD) – usually known as the World Bank.

International Development Association (IDA) – a division of the World Bank that provides highly concessional loans to countries that fall below a certain income level; conditionalities are imposed.

International Development Goals (IDGs) – the targets for reduction in poverty and improvements of health, education, gender equality and environmental protection by the year 2005 agreed by the OECD.

International financial architecture – grandiose name for the ad-hoc system of global surveillance, standard- setting and regulation governing international capital flows.

International financial institutions (IFIs) – the World Bank, IMF and regional development banks, like the Inter-American Development Bank.

International Monetary Fund (IMF) – established in 1944 to promote international monetary co-operation and short-term balance of payment assistance with macro-economic structural adjustments imposed; increasing taking on other roles.

Liberalisation – reducing/removing government controls on the price of goods and services and/or reducing/removing taxes or other trade barriers on imports and exports and other financial transactions.

London Club – a group of commercial bankers who meet to restructure loans owed by governments experiencing debt service problems; often require an IMF SAP and Paris Club agreement in place.

Macro-economic – pertaining to the performance or interaction of aggregate economic indicators, such as: investment, taxation, government spending, money supply, exports, imports, interest and exchange rates.

Macro-economic and structural reform programmes – economic policies required by the World Bank and the IMF as a condition for their loans, usually with regard to balance of payments, fiscal deficit, money supply and inflation.

Millennium Round – first trade negotiations of the WTO, in abeyance.

Multi-lateral financial institutions (MDBs) – Intergovernmental finance and development agencies.

Multi-national corporation (MNC) – also known as trans-national corporations (see TNC).

Moral hazard – the danger that a policy measure will have a counterproductive effect on the incentives facing market players.

Moratorium – When a debtor temporarily suspends debt service payments

Net present value (NPV) – the amount of money which would need to be invested at a commercial interest rate at the beginning of the period of debt repayments, such that with accumulated interest, it would be just adequate to meet all the payments as they fall due.

Non-governmental organisations (NGOs) – not for profit or voluntary organisations.

North – Industrialised developed countries.

North American Free Trade Agreement (NAFTA) – a trade and investment agreement among the US, Canada and Mexico.

Official debt – owed to public creditors such as governments, MDBs and the IMF.

OPEC – Organization of Petroleum Exporting Countries.

Organisation for Economic Co-operation and Development (OECD) – represents the 29 most industrialised countries.

Paris Club – the major forum for rescheduling official debt.

Petrodollars – money earned from OPEC oil sales and deposited in Northern banks.

Protectionism – a variety of government policies to protect domestic industries from foreign competition.

South – Used to be referred to as the Third World.

Restructured debt (also rescheduled) – When an outstanding loan is revised at a lower interest rate and/or a longer repayment period.

Sovereign loans – loans to national governments.

Structural Adjustment Loans(SALs)/Programmes (SAPs) – balance of payment loans that are given to governments for budget support but conditioned on policy changes.

Subsidiarity – delegating as much responsibility as possible to the lowest appropriate administrative level.

Terms of trade – the ratio between the average price of exports and the average price of imports, expressed as an index; shows how much a country can buy abroad for each unit of export sales.

Third World – Developing or 'underdeveloped' countries (see South).

Total debt – the total amount a country owes.

Total debt service (TDS) – the sum of the interest and capital repayments made in a given year.

Transparency – open and accountable processes of governance and finance that are accessible to the public.

Trillion – US and Canada, a million million. Britain, France, Germany, a million, million, million.

UN Conference on Trade and Development (UNCTAD) – main objective is to promote trade and investment, with special attention to the developing countries.

Uruguay Round – last round of GATT trade negotiations.

US General Accounting Office (GAO) – an investigative arm of the US Congress charges with examining matters relating to the receipt of public funds.

Write-off (also debt cancellation)- When a creditor takes an unpaid debt off the 'books' no longer expecting payment.

World Trade Organisation (WTO) – a specialised agency responsible for negotiations on international rules concerning trade.

# Relevant web sites

- **Alternative Information and Development Centre** – South Africa
  http://www.aidc.org.za
  Alternative information centre doing research, education and training
  as well as campaigning and lobbying on the macro-issues affecting the
  development process in South Africa (good links for other geographic
  regions)
- **Bank Information Center** – USA
  http://www.bicusa.org
  BIC is an independent, non-profit NGO that provides information
  and strategic support to NGOs and social movements throughout the
  world on projects, policies and practices of the World Bank and other
  MDBs. BIC advocates for greater transparency, accountability and
  citizen participation at the MDBs
- **Bretton Woods Project** – England
  http://www.brettonwoodsproject.org
  Works to monitor and reform the World Bank and IMF, tracking key
  policy statements and reports and provides critiques and early warnings
  used by NGOs across the world
- **Catholic Fund for Overseas Development (CAFOD)** – England
  http://www.cafod.org.uk
  One of the UK's leading development and relief organisations – a voice
  for the poor, raising awareness of the causes of poverty and injustice.
  Policy analysis and advocacy on WTO, debt and other related issues
- **Center of Concern** -USA
  http://www.coc.org/coc
  Works with international networks promoting social analysis, theologi-
  cal reflection, policy analysis, political advocacy research and public
  education on issues of global development, peace and social justice
- **Christian Aid** – UK
  http://www.christian-aid.org
  see CAFOD above – similar coverage
- **Development Group for Alternative Policies (D-GAP)** – USA
  http://www.developmentgap.org
  Since 1977 the D-GAP has worked to ensure that the knowledge,
  priorities and efforts of the women and men of the South inform
  decisions made in the North about their economies and the environment in which they live. Through its collaboration with citizens'

organizations around the world, the D-GAP is able to demonstrate practical alternatives to prevailing policies and programs. Currently undertaking the SAPRIN (Structural Adjustment Participatory Review International Network) exercise, which in Latin America includes Ecuador, El Salvador and Mexico

- **Ecumenical Coalition for Economic Justice (GATTFLY)** – Canada
  http://www.ecej.org
  A project of the Canadian Churches working together for a just, moral and sustainable 'economy of hope,' inspired by the biblical vision of Jubilee. Conducts research and policy analysis, education and leadership development, advocacy and linking to social justice movements
- **European Network on Debt and Development (EURODAD)** – Belgium
  http://www.oneworld.org/eurodad
  A network of NGOs in 16 European countries, it aims to coordinate the activities of NGOs working on the issues of Third World debt, structural adjustment and financial markets in order to ensure that their views are brought to bear on decision-makers in Europe, the BWIs and other relevant players
- **Fifty (50) Years is Enough: US Network for Global Economic Justice** – USA
  http://www.50years.org
  A coalition of over 200 grassroots, faith-based, policy, women's, social- and economic justice, youth, solidarity, labor and development organizations dedicated to the profound transformation of the World Bank and IMF. Was formed on the occasion of the 50th anniversary of the founding of the World Bank/IMF
- **Foreign Policy in Focus (InterHemispheric Research Center and Institute for Policy Studies)** -USA
  http://www.foreignpolicy-infocus.org
  Much on World Trade Organisation and other related subjects
- **Focus on the Global South** - Thailand (Walden Bello)
  http://www.focusweb.org
  Focus is a project of progressive development policy research and practice, dedicated to regional and global policy analysis, micro-macro linking and advocacy work. Focus works with NGOs and people's organizations in the Asia Pacific and other regions
- **Friends of the Earth (FOE)** – USA
  http://www.foe.org
  FOE is an environmental organization dedicated to preserving the health and diversity of the planet for future generations. As the largest

international network in the world, with affiliates in 63 countries, FOE empowers citizens to have an influential voice in decisions affecting their environment and their lives

- **Institute for Agricultural and Trade Policy** – USA
  http://www.iatp.org
  IATP's mission is to create environmentally and economically sustainable rural communities and regions through sound agricultural and trade policy. Assist public interest organizations in coalition building and influencing both domestic (US) and international policymaking through monitoring, analysis and research, education and outreach, and information systems management
- **Jubilee South**
  http://www.jubileesouth.net
  Jubilee South is a coalition of Jubilee Debt Campaigns and social movements from Africa, Asia, Latin America and the Caribbean
- **Jubilee 2000-USA** – USA
  http://www.j2000usa.org/j2000
- **Jubilee 2000-UK** – England
  http://www.oneworld.org/jubilee2000
  or http://www.jubilee2000uk.org
  Jubilee 2000 is an international movement in over 40 countries advocating a debt free start to the new Millennium to benefit over 1billion people – J2K-UK was one of the first to organize
- **International Monetary Fund** – USA
  http://www.imf.org
- **OXFAM/America** – USA
  http://www.oxfamamerica.org
- **OXFAM International**
  http://www.oxfaminternational.org
- **OXFAM/UK**
  http://www.oxfam.org.uk
- **Preamble Center** – USA
  http://www.preamble.org
  An independent research and public education organization that works in partnership with a broad network of academics, policy professionals and community leaders who share concerns about the pressing social, economic and political challenges facing the world
- **Third World Network** – Malaysia (Martin Kohr)
  http://www.twnside.org.sg
  An independent, non-profit, international network of organisations and individuals involved in issues relating to development, the Third

World and North-South topics

- **TransNational Institute (TNI)** – Netherlands
  http://www.tni.org
  An international network of activist-scholars concerned with analysing
  and finding viable solutions to global problems – has a WTO project
- **Uganda Debt Network** – Uganda
  http://www.uganda.co.ug/debt
  To advocate for reduced and sustainable debt levels, accountability and
  effective use of national resources for the benefit of all people of
  Uganda (with Jubilee2000-Uganda, carrying out a multi-year civil
  society transparency campaign, considered by many to be the best in
  the world)
- **World Bank**
  http://www.worldbank.org
- **WDM**
  http://www.wdm.org.uk/action/debt.htm
- **World Trade Organisation** – Switzerland
  http://www.wto.org
- **World Trade Organisation Watch** – USA
  http://www.wtowatch.org
  Excellent source of critical information on the WTO

# Bibliography

Acknowledgements and permissions
The author thanks all those who have made material available for inclusion.
All attemps have been made to clear permissions with copyright holders.
All translations are by the author unless otherwise specified.

Alliance for Responsible Trade, A Manifesto,
  at http://www.igc.org/dgap/art/artwhatfor.html
Ambrose, Soren *In Focus: Multilateral Debt*, at http://www.foreignpolicy-
  infocus.org/, 1999.
Bank Information Center, *Headlines of the 1999 WB/IMF Annual
  Meetings*, Washington DC, October, 1999.
Barkin, David, 'Free Trade and Environmental Policymaking in Mexico,'
  *The Progressive Response*, Vol.3 #36
Barry, Tom, ed., *Foreign Policy in Focus*, Progressive Response, New
  Mexico, 1999.
Bello, Walden, *Dark Victory: The United States, Structural Adjustment and
  Global Poverty*, Pluto Press, London, 1994.
*The Iron Cage: The WTO, The Bretton Woods Institutions, and the South*,
  Focus on Trade, #41, Focus on the Global South, Thailand, November
  1999.
Bendaña, Alejandro, 'Which way NGOs?' in *Bulletin of the Interhemi-
  spheric Resource Center*, No.51, 1998.
Berneria, Lourdes and M.J. Dudley, *Economic Restructuring in the
  Americas*, Latin America Studies Program Cornell University,
  Occasional Papers Studies, Vol. 3, Ithaca, New York, 1996.
Block, Donna, *Abracadabra Says the IMF: Plan to Fund Debt Relief to
  Poorer Nations by Revaluing Its Gold Stash Is Just Smoke and Mirrors*,
  Mail and Guardian Debt News Today (via email), October, 1999.
Boyd, Stephanie, Debt Crisis, *Latinamerica Press*, (special issue), 20
  December 1999, Vol. 31, No. 47
Bread for the World Institute, *Debt and Development DOSSIER*, Issues #1
  & #2 September 1999.
Bretton Woods Committee on the Process Towards a New Financial
  Architecture (First Report), *An International Economic Challenge: The
  Complexity of Capital Mobility*, Australia National University, Canberra,
  Australia, July, 1999.
Bretton Woods Project, *The Bank's New Framework: Opportunities and
  Omissions*, London, September, 1999.

Campos, Urbano, 'Globalización y suicidio,' *Los Tiempos*, Cochabamba, Bolivia, December 14, 1999.

CEPAL, *Anuario Estadístico de América Latina y el Caribe*, Chile, 1999.

Conger, Lucy, 'As Ecuador Tarries, Financiers Fret,' *Emerging Markets IMF/World Bank Daily*, September 27 1999.

'Ecuadoran Bradys: How Far Will the Fallout Spread?' *Emerging Markets IMF/World Bank Daily*, September 26, 1999.

'Mexican Banks: Where the Money Isn't,' *Emerging Markets IMF/World Bank Daily*, September 26 1999.

Council on Foreign Relations, *Safeguarding Prosperity in a Global Financial System: The Future Financial Architecture Report of an Independent Task Force*, New York, 1999.

Christian Aid, Who Owes Who? Policy report, 1999.

De Young, Karen, 'Generosity Shrinks in an Age of Prosperity,' *Guardian Weekly*, December 2-8 1999.

Dillon, John, *Investment, Finance and Debt in the Americas: A Document Prepared by the Hemispheric Social Alliance for the Americas Civil Society Forum*, Ecumenical Coalition for Economic Justice, Toronto, November, 1998.

Esteva, Gustavo, multiple personal correspondence, 1999.

Esteva, Gustavo and M. Prakesh, 'Beyond Development, What?', *Development in Practice*, Oxfam, Vol.8 #3, Oxford, 1998a.

*Grassroots Post-Modernism: Remaking the Soil of Cultures*, Zed, London, 1998b.

EURODAD, *Summary Analysis of the G7 Cologne Summit*, July, 1999.

50 Years is Enough, *Africa Needs Debt Cancellation*, Washington, DC, 1998.

García, Alan, *La Década Infame*, on the internet at http://www.geocities.com/alangarcia_2000/, 1999.

Gariyo, Zie, *Uganda HIPC Experience and Development-Oriented Borrowing*, presentation by the Uganda Debt Network at EURODAD Annual Meeting, Italy, 1998.

Green, Duncan, *Capital Punishment: Making International Finance Work for the World's Poor*, CAFOD, London, England, September, 1999.

Haiti Rebound Update, Quixote Center, Washington DC, 1999.

Hanlon, Joseph, *HIPC Heresies and the Flat Earth Response*, Jubilee 2000 Coalition, London, 1998a.

*We've Been Here Before: Debt, Default and Relief in the Past – and How We are Demanding That the Poor Pay More This Time*, Jubilee 2000 Coalition, London, 1998b.

Hansen-Kuhn, Karen, 'Free Trade Area of the Americas,' *In Focus*, Vol.3

#6, Washington D.C., April 1998.

Hernandez, Max and Malcolm Rodgers, *Hurricane Mitch Hits Honduras*, Christian Aid, London, October, 1999.

Hunter, David and Van Dyke, Brennan 'Trade and Environment,' *The Progressive Response,* Vol.3 #36, via internet, 8 October 1999.

Iriarte, Gregorio, *Análisis Crítico de la Realidad,* CEPROMI, Cochabamba, Bolivia, 1999.

Jordan, Lisa, *The Death of Development? The Converging Policy Agendas of the World Bank and the World Trade Organization,* Bank Information Center, Washington, DC, November 1999.

Jubilee 2000/USA, *Responses to the Debt Crisis,* Washington DC, 1998.

Jubilee 2000 Coalition, *The Facts,* London, n.d.

Jubilee 2000/LatinAmerica & Caribbean, *Yes to Life, No to Death* Platform Declaration, Honduras, January 1999.
*For a Debt Free Millennium: Buenos Aires Declaration,* Argentina, September, 1999.

Jubilee 2000-UK, *Basic Data on 92 Poorest Countries,* London, 1999.

Jubilee 2000/USA, *Responses to the Debt Crisis,* Washington DC, 1998.

Juniper, Tony, 'Planet Profit,' *Guardian Weekly,* London, 11/25-12/1, 1999.

LatinAmerica Press, *Special Issue on the Debt Crisis,* Peru, December, 1999

Lockwood, Matthew and A. Wood, *The 'Perestroika of Aid'? New Perspectives on Conditionality,* Christian Aid and Bretton Woods Project, London, 1999.

McGowan, Lisa, *Bailouts for Bankers, Burdens for Women,* 50 Years is Enough, Washington, DC, 1998a.
*Corporate Welfare in Haiti,* 50 Years is Enough, Washington, DC, 1998b.

OXFAM International, *Outcome of IMF/World Bank September 1999 Annual Meeting: Poverty Reduction and Debt Relief,* Washington DC, November 1999.

OXFAM and UNICEF, *Debt Relief and Poverty Reduction: Meeting the Challenge,* via internet, 1999.

Petras, James, 'The Left Strikes Back: Class Conflict in Latin America in the Age of Neoliberalism', *Latin American Perspectives* Series No.19, Westview Press, Oxford, UK, 1999.

Potter, George Ann, *Dialogue on Debt: Alternative Analyses and Solutions,* Center of Concern, Washington DC, 1988.

Reed, David, *Structural Adjustment, the Environment and Sustainable Development,* Island Press, Washington D.C., 1996.

Rich, Bruce, *The Challenge of Social and Environmental Sustainability; The*

*Case of Export Credit Agencies*, EURODAD Annual Meeting, Italy, 1998.

Ross, John, 'Mexico: Fallout From the "Battle of Seattle,"' *LatinAmerica Press*, Peru, December, 1999.

Saavedra, Luis Angel, Debt Crisis, *Latinamerica Press*, (special issue), December 20 1999, Vol. 31, No. 47

Sachs, Jeffrey, *Testimony on International Debt Before the US House Banking Committee*, Washington DC, June, 15 1999.

Schamis, Hector, E, 'The Politics of Economic Reform in Latin America: Collective Action, Institution Building, and the State,' in Berneria and Dudley.

Shiva, Vandana, *The Historic Significance of Seattle,* from the Development GAP personal email, 1999.

Standard and Poor's Credit Week, 'Mexican Banks: Bailout Costs Continue to Rise,' August 25 1999.

The Economist, *Special: The Non-Governmental Order: Will NGOs Democratise, or Merely Disrupt, Global Governance?*, London, 12/11-17, 1999.

Ugarteche, Oscar, 'Exclusión: La Otra Cara de la Globalizatión,' *America Latina En Movimiento*, ALAI, Ecuador, September 29, 1999.

'The Structural Adjustment Stranglehold,' *NACLA*, Vol.XXXIII, #1, July/August 1999.

United Nations, *World Economic and Social Survey 1998: Trends and Policies in the World Economy*, UN, New York, 1998.

United Nations Development Program (UNDP), *Informe Sobre Desarrollo Humano 1999*, UNDP, New York, 1999.

Veltmeyer, Henry, James Petras and Steve Vieux, *Neoliberalism and Class Conflict in Latin America: A Comparative Perspective on the Political Economy of Strucutral Adjustment*, International Political Economy Series, Macmillan, England, nd.

Watkins, Kevin, *Globalisation and Liberalisation: Implications for Poverty, Distribution and Inequality*, UNDP, New York, 1997.

Willoughby, Jack and Lucy Conger, 'Under the Volcano,' *Institutional Investor*, June 1998.

Wood, Angela, personal correspondence with the author during 1999.

Woodward, David, *Drowning By Numbers: The IMF, The World Bank and North-South Financial Flows*, Bretton Woods Project, London, 1998.

World Bank, *Bolivia Country Assessment Strategy*, 1998.

*World Development Report on Poverty-Consultation Draft*, available on World Bank web site, January 2000.

# Index